AVX

JENNIFER JULIE MILLER

ACKNOWLEDGMENTS

I want to dedicate this book to my husband, **Rick.** There are no words to describe my love for you, but the one thing I really want to say is, thank you, for WANTING me, and for being my HERO!

Also, I want to say thanks to my parents, my amazing kids, my beautiful grandkids, my crazy aunt, and all my friends for all your constant support. I want to thank my family for all the hours you have had to listen to the insane ideas inside my head. Even though most of you think I need to be evaluated.

Kindle & Paperback Edition:

This is an original work of

Jennifer Julie Miller

All rights reserved.

No part of this publication may be used or reproduced or transmitted in any manner whatsoever, electronically, in print, or otherwise, without written permission from the author, except in the case of brief quotations embodied in critical articles and reviews.

This book is a work of fiction. The names, characters, places, and incidents are the products of the writer's imagination. Any resemblance to actual persons, living or dead, business establishments, events, or locales is entirely coincidental.

COPYRIGHT

Copyright: © 2022 Jennifer Julie Miller

Cover Art by © **Creative cover Designs (Vicki Adrian) Artist.**

Beta Readers:

Lorene Palmer, Rick Miller, Ethel Nance.

Editors:

Partners in Crime Book Services, Randy Henry

Photographs:

Brittany Henry & Rick Miller, Shutterstock

Imaginational inspiration crew:

Diamond Shipman, Amanda Hall, Joann Herley, Vicki Adrian.

CHAPTER 1

I^{vy}

"Dammit, Mom! Lord, I'm so sick and tired of us arguing non-stop. I swear you are the most negative person I know,… there are times I think you hate air! I wish, just once, that you could understand how bad I want something else for my life. But we have had this argument over and over again and I know it's never going to matter what I say. We are simply not going to agree.

"I have come to realize a long time ago you are never going to agree to anything that wasn't your idea first. With that being said, stop yelling at me and listen to the words coming out of my mouth. I'm not staying here another minute, no matter how loudly you object, or how mad you get at me."

Pulling my favorite clothes out of the closet, I turn around, facing her. "Why is it so hard for you to fathom that I don't want to be trapped in this one-horse town working at the local burger joint for the rest of my life? All of that may be ok for you, but it's not for me. Not only that, but shit, I'm sick and tired of our constant fighting. If I didn't look so much like you, I would swear I was switched at birth. For you to be my mother, we have nothing in common.

"I don't understand why it angers you so badly that I want more? Why can't you be happy for me for once? You know, be a normal parent and encourage me to make the step you were never brave enough to do yourself. This is my only opportunity to get out of here, and I can't pass it by because you think the timing is wrong. If I wait until all the stars line up, I'll never leave here. Sometimes I swear you act like a complete stranger to me. What mother wants her child to settle for less?"

I stomp around this pathetic area I call a bedroom, filling my bag up with what few items I have worth anything while Mom watches me from the doorway.

"Hell, Mom, we both know the only reason you have not pushed me out the door already is because of what little money I do make... I give half to you. I mean, what future do I have here? We live in bum fucked Egypt, in a beat-up old trailer with one vehicle. I mean, for god's sake, we don't even have cell phones because neither of us can pay the bill. I'm living a rerun of your life and I want out.

"Being my mother, you should want me to be more, have more. Instead, all I am is an extra set of hands and now an added income. I have been out of high school for almost two years, and every time I mention I want to get a place of my own, or hell, how about a car? All I get from you is negativity. Do you really want the life you have lived for me too? I can't help it that Dad walked off and that every guy you have dated since has been a piece of shit. But that's you, Mom, not me! Why should your bad decisions affect the rest of my life, too?"

Mom stands in the doorway, her hands on her hips, red-faced and mad at me as usual. "Ivy… I know you believe this boy is the answer to all your problems. But are you really that naïve? How can you possibly believe this kid is just gonna magically give you everything you want? He is nothing but a loser, and a punk who thinks the whole world owes him something. He is lying to your face and you are too gullible to see it. You want out so badly you are willing to jump at anything by this point. There is no way he has family clear across the country that is going to take you in for free. People never give you anything for nothing, and I believe this is going to be a hard lesson learned.

"You're a beautiful girl, Ivy. Your whole life is still ahead of you. No, I don't want you living my life. That's why I'm trying to talk some sense into you right now. I know you think I'm holding you back, but I'm simply trying to keep you safe. What's going to happen is…you're going to get away from home where you have no one but him to depend on. Then he is going to leave your ass at some random place in the middle of the night. Probably because most of the time you're a little bitch who is never satisfied and he will be sick and tired of listening to your mouth. He is going to abandon you, Ivy…leaving you with no way to get home. Then, because you're stuck without a dime to your name…you're gonna end up having to make a living on your back. At least here you have a chance. You can go to college. Possibly, find a guy who wants something, someone you can build your life with. You need to get away from your so-called friends, not where you live, if you want something more.

"You think I'm using you? It's nothing compared to what he is going to do. He is taking you away from me and everything you know. You know I don't have the resources to help you if you get in trouble nine states away. I'm barely making the rent and utilities now, even with your help. If you get hurt, I can't come get you. Here we at least have each other."

I throw the bag down on the bed and turn back to her, practically screaming. "What do you want me to do, Mom? Just stay here and wilt away like you have? Watch all my dreams fade with my looks? Hope that some random guy passing through this two-bit town notices me? Or how about this? The highlight of my life is…now wait for it… I make it to supervisor after ten years of working at the burger world. I'm leaving and there is nothing you can do about it. I refuse to become anything like you and if I stay, that's exactly what is going to happen. You are living proof of what waiting for something better is. I am going to make something out of myself, with or without your approval. Why can't you be supportive for once?"

My mom shakes her head. "Because I know what's out there and you don't. The moment you walk out that door, I will never see you again. You have grown up in a town with two red lights, Ivy. You have no idea how to function in a big city. They are going to chew you up and spit you out. Believe it or not, at one time I knew everything, too. Things are not great here and I wish I had the answers or the means to give you the life you crave, but baby, this is not the route you need to go."

A horn blows outside and I zip my bag up, throwing it over my shoulder. "Look, Mom, I'll try to call, like from a pay phone or something, when I can, but I'm leaving. I love you and I appreciate the mom stuff, but I refuse to spend the best years of my life in a place where I have no future."

As I walk past her into the hallway, I bite my lip, trying not to cry. I'm not only mad at her, but I'm hurt, too. So many times she could have left this place, but she refused to leave because of all the unknowns. I know what my future holds here: I won't have one. Worst-case scenario, I end up back here in a few years, living the same miserable life she has.

Tommy honks the horn again as I'm walking out the front door. He opens the passenger door from the inside and I throw my bag in the back.

"You ready to go?"

"Oh, yeah."

"That bad, huh? The same old, same old."

"You know it." I wipe a tear off my cheek as I look through the car mirror at Mom standing on the front porch watching us drive away. I should have hugged her before I left, but if I stop this car and go back now, I might stay.

Tommy turns the radio up as we get on the interstate and the farther I get from home, the heavier my heart feels. Mom's words play over in my mind. I tell myself I'll call her at the next rest area and apologize. Then I push those thoughts away and watch the scenery as it goes by. Praying that, for once, Mom is wrong.

By the time we stop for gas later, my legs are stiff from sitting in the car for so long. I get out, stretching as Tommy fills the gas tank. A group of guys in a truck whistle and honk their horn as they go by. I turn my head away, not wanting to encourage them further.

I look over at Tommy to see if he is going to say anything, but he never has been the jealous type. We're not really girlfriend and boyfriend, more like two kids trying to escape the world we were both born into.

He puts the nozzle back and turns towards me before he heads into the store. "You want anything?"

"Nah I'm good, thanks. If you are going to be a minute, there is a payphone over there. I'm gonna call Mom real quick...forgot to tell her something."

"Go ahead, I'm in zero hurry. You wanna use my phone?"

I shake my head no. "I bought a calling card, but thanks." The sad part as I watch him walk away is that I know I don't love him, and probably never will. If I'm even truer to myself, I can probably admit that I'm not attracted to him anymore, either. Since we were kids, we have always been a thing. We grew up next to each other, and he has just always been there. Now, that I take a second to think about it, the only thing we have in common is the need to escape the world we were born into.

We have become so obsessed about leaving, I believe we may have lost ourselves in the process. So many nights we sat doing nothing but talking about the what ifs and the possibilities of being somewhere else. I used to tease him that we were like two people dreaming of winning the lottery. All the things we could do if we just had some extra money. Tommy and I both have been saving every dime we could for what feels like years now. So when the opportunity arose, we could just leave. I have worked so many doubles lately that not being at work feels weird. Not only is my body tired, but so is my mind. And this fight with mom isn't helping me any.

I don't know who was more shocked, Tommy or me, when his cousin told us on the phone the other night that he would put us up for a few months until we could get on our feet. Said they had an extra bedroom, and that there were jobs everywhere. He even sent us a couple of links for jobs to apply for before we get out there. When Tommy got an interview request almost immediately from one of the biggest plants out there at the end of the week, I don't know who was more shocked. I'm overwhelmed by the unknowns coming our way. I have so many questions running through my head. But it doesn't do me any good to ask Tommy because he doesn't know any more than I do.

Tommy has become comfortable and even if things don't work out between us as time goes on, at least by then I'll know more about my surroundings and possibly other opportunities. Even though Mom thinks he is a loser because he didn't want to go to college or work his dad's farm, Tommy is a great guy. Unfortunately, there is just no spark between us anymore.

I shake the thoughts away, blaming my melancholy on the fight I had with Mom before we left. I grab my bag out of the back and my wallet so I can use the calling card I bought and walk around the building. It takes me a few times to get all the numbers in, but finally, the call goes through. The phone rings what feels like a dozen times before mom finally picks up.

"Mom, it's me. I just wanted to say I'm sorry again. I feel terrible leaving like that." I no longer get that out, that a horn honks behind me. It's those guys in the truck again.

"Hey, pretty thing, you need a ride?" the driver yells out.

"Mom, hold on a second."

I point toward the phone and shake my head. "No, I'm good, but thanks for the offer."

"Ivy, why would they be asking you that?"

"Not sure, honestly." I try to look back toward the pumps where Tommy's car is, but I can't see it from here.

The driver turns to look at the other guys in the truck with him. "Mom, I better go. I think these guys have been drinking or something, and Tommy is probably waiting for me back at the car, just wanted to say, I love ya."

"Ivy, before you hang up, do you know where you're at?"

"I think we are getting ready to cross into Illinois." Tommy pulls up beside the phone booth and I can hear him and the guys in the truck start shouting back and forth at each other.

"Come on, Ivy!" I hear Tommy yell.

"Mom, I'll try to call again later when we stop for the night." I hang up the phone before she can say anything else. Tommy gets out of the car and motions for me to slide in through from his side. The guys in the truck are making obscene gestures as they yell out all the vulgar things they want to do to me.

Tommy gets back in and starts to back the car out. And just as he does, the other guy slams his truck in reverse, trying to block us in. I scream when the truck clips us in the front. Tommy doesn't stop, though. He whips the car around quickly, and we head back towards the main road. I stick my head out the window and yell back. "What the fuck is your problem?"

"Don't encourage them, Ivy. I'm highly outnumbered."

"Why in the hell are they acting like this? Do you think they hurt your car?"

"You must have looked like easy prey, or maybe they're on something. They hit us, but I don't think it was hard enough to do much damage. Just keep a lookout until we get a few hundred miles away from here, then I'll get out and check the car."

I am starting to relax when the car begins making a squealing noise. Tommy goes to slow down and just as he begins to pull over to the side of the road, something under the car gives out and we slide hard into the berm, hitting the guardrail. I'm jerked forward, my head hitting the dash before I can stop myself.

Tommy grabs me the moment the car stops. "Are you ok?"

I rub the little knot forming on my forehead. "Yeah, just knocked me silly there for a second." I reach up, wiping the blood off his face, and then grab my bag, pulling a tissue out of the side pocket. "Here, your cheek is bleeding. Are you hurt anywhere else?"

He shakes his head. "It knocked the air out of me, but other than that, I think I'm ok. Let me catch my breath and then I'll go see how bad it is."

I try to get my door open, only to find it stuck. "I can't get out on my side."

He hits the steering wheel. "Man, this is just our fucking luck. It's going to cost a fortune to have this car towed somewhere. Stay here."

He gets out and walks around the car and when he puts his head down, cussing. I know it's bad. I try to roll the window down, but it isn't working either. Tommy comes back around and plops back into the driver's seat, looking over at me.

"How bad is it?"

"Apparently, those dicks did more damage than I thought. Fuck, I knew I should have gotten out and checked sooner." He hits the dash. "When they hit us, it must have pushed the fender in, and it has been rubbing against the tire this whole time."

"Can we pull it back out, then change the tire?"

"That would have been a possibility, but that was the spare. And…we hit the road so hard it bent the rim. I knew I should have got that fixed before we left, but I was trying to save every dime I could. I can't imagine what a tire and new rim are going to cost. Man, I really hate to call my dad. I have had enough *you're going to fail* speeches to last me a lifetime here lately."

"Same here, so what do we do? Can we possibly get another wheel at a junkyard?"

"Maybe, let me look it up and see if there are any around us." He pulls his cell phone out, moving it around. Then he shakes his head and starts to laugh. "We have no service, doesn't that figure… Looks like we're walking."

CHAPTER 2

I vy

WE PULL a few things out of the car and head down the road on foot. There is absolutely nothing around us for miles but cotton fields. Thankfully, the moon is bright in the sky and it's relatively warm out. There have been a few cars going by and even though we talked about it, we decided not to take the chance on hitchhiking. There has to be a farm or a town within the next few miles.

I notice that the longer we walk, the slower Tommy seems to be getting. Several times now I have seen him grab his side. "Hey, you wanna take a break?"

"Sorry, but man, I feel like shit all of a sudden, my ribs are killing me. I knew I hit the steering wheel pretty hard, but now I'm beginning to wonder if I may have broken something. Let's stop for a second and let me catch my breath."

We walk over to the guardrail and lean up against it. I take the bottle of water I have in my bag out and give it to him.

"Thanks, I needed this. I swear, even in school, you had the magic bag."

"All girls need survival kits. That's something we learn early in life. Check your phone and see if we have any service yet."

He pulls it out of his back pocket and holds it up. "Yessss, one bar. I still don't know if I should call my dad or a tow truck."

"We were going to find a cheap motel tonight, anyway. Use that money and call the tow truck. Hopefully, they will know where to take the car to get it fixed. I'm sure they won't leave us out here and will let us ride along. Once we get there, we will just sleep in the car."

He looks at me for a second. "See, that's why I have kept you all these years. Not only are you beautiful, but you're also smart."

"Yeah, yeah, you tell all the girls that.

"Maybe, but those other girls are not the ones walking with me down the road in the middle of nowhere. You are, so you're stuck with me."

Playfully, I smack his arm. "I have always been stuck with you. All the other guys thought you were going to beat them up if they even talked to me."

"You're my girl. They had no reason to talk to you."

"Possessive much!"

"Nah, just can't imagine a day that you weren't in it. You are like that old favorite shirt I never leave home without."

"Wow, what a romantic."

"Yeah, I'm not very good at all that stuff, but you know I adore you. Our lives were being pulled apart back home, but now, it's just us against the world. This rough spot will pass and, in a few months, I'll be coming home to you. In our own place, with your fine cooking."

"My fine cooking. What, Steakums and shells and cheese?"

"Hey, as long as it's cooked in our place, I don't give a shit." He walks around while he tries several numbers. Finally, I can hear him talking to someone. "Mile marker, I'm not sure. Ivy, have you noticed any mile markers as we have been walking?"

"Yeah, one eighty-seven."

He rattles it off to the guy and then hangs up the phone, cussing again. "Dammit, he said he can't come until morning. Apparently, we are in the middle of nowhere. I should have noticed that there have only been a few cars going by the last few hours."

"But he is coming?"

"He said he was."

"Well, let's head back to the car then. We were going to sleep in it either way, and I would be more comfortable locked inside it than out here in a field somewhere." We start back down the road and I swear it seems like we have been walking forever. Both of us are so drained that we are just making ourselves take one step in front of the other.

"Tommy, did the damn car get stolen or something? I don't remember walking this far."

"I think it's just around this next bend, but I thought the same thing about the last two. If it's not, I'm going to have to sit down. I feel like I'm smothering."

I turn around and wait until he is next to me before I tuck myself up under his arm. "Here, lean on me some. You don't have to play tough guy out here, no one can see."

He pulls me close and laughs. "I will deny every word if you tell anyone."

I see the lights before I see the car. At first, I thought it might be the cops or even a tow truck by the way they were using a spotlight to look around. When the light settles on us, I hold my hand up over my eyes, blocking the intense beams. Suddenly doors are slamming and that's when I hear them. It's the guys from the gas station.

We stop walking instantly. I look around, knowing there is no escaping them on foot. "Ivy, I will try to distract them. You need to run. Hide in a culvert or something. These guys are up to no good."

"Absolutely not, and this is not me arguing with you. I agree with you for a change, but there is nowhere out here that they can't find me. I'm safer with you."

Apparently, the driver is the leader because they all stand behind him as he walks toward us. "Well, what do we have here? It's sweet thing and her man? What's the odds that we would find you two out here all alone?"

Tommy unwinds himself from me and pushes me behind him. "Look buddy, we don't want any trouble. We are just passing through."

The guy sneers at Tommy. "Seems like you already found yourself in a bit of trouble. Your car appears to be beaten up and you're not doing much better from the looks of it."

Tommy doesn't back down as the guys start to spread out around us. "The cops and the tow truck are on their way. We had to walk up the road to get a signal, but they should be here anytime."

The guy spits on the ground as he shakes his head. "There is nothing I hate any worse than a liar, country boy. My uncle owns the tow company you called, and he is three sheets to the wind right now, drunk." He motions to the guys with him. "We might be persuaded to help you guys out, though."

"I appreciate the offer, but we don't have any money or anything else to offer you. Why don't you guys go on about your business and just leave us alone?"

The guys all start laughing. "I think we might be having a misunderstanding, country boy. I don't believe we were asking. You send sweet thing on over here and see if she can do a better job convincing us to help you guys out."

"She isn't an option."

He no more says that when someone grabs me from behind, picking me up off my feet. Tommy turns lunging towards the guy who grabbed me, only for the other guys to jump on him when he turned his back to them.

The guy holding me licks the side of my face as I kick and squirm, trying to loosen my arms he has pinned to my sides. I scream Tommy's name when I see one of them knock him to the ground, then they all start kicking him in the side.

"Stop it, you're going to kill him."

The leader puts his hand up and they all step back away from Tommy, only to turn toward me. I stop fighting the guy who has been holding me and he sets me on my feet in front of him, still gripping me with my arms pinned down to my sides. The leader walks calmly up to me. I see his beady eyes raking me up and down. His face is scarred, and he is slightly shorter than I am with greasy blond hair. They all smell heavily of beer.

He reaches out to touch my face and I bite at his fingers. "Don't touch me!" The guys with him start to laugh. Teasing him about a county girl getting the best of him. He backhands me. My head hits the guy's chest behind me hard, and blood pools inside my mouth where my teeth had cut the inside of my cheek. I spit the blood out, barely missing the leader's shoes. He grabs me by my hair, pulling my face up close to his.

"You like to spit huh, well let's put that mouth of yours to work." He starts yanking at the zipper on his jeans as the guy who had been holding me this whole time kicks the back of my legs and I hit the ground hard. But when he pushes me down, I managed to pull one of my hands free. The leader grabs my hair, pulling me forward towards his crotch. I grab onto the leader's dick and twist hard. Screaming, he starts hitting me on top of my head and shoulders, trying to free himself, but I simply squeeze and twist harder.

"Get her off me!" I can hear him yelling at his friends for someone to help him, but none of them jump to his rescue immediately. He is practically on his knees when I see one of them headed toward us. I let go and push him into them and turn to run, only to be tackled to the ground. My head hits the pavement so hard I almost black out.

Multiple hands grab at my clothes. I can hear my shirt ripping as I try to fight them off. Tommy screams out my name, then a gun goes off. Everyone suddenly stops. I drag myself along the road, pushing myself to my feet. Wiping the blood out of my eyes, only to look back long enough to see Tommy… laying in a puddle of blood, half of his face missing. A sob escapes my throat when I realize what they have done. If they will do that to him, what will they do to me? My head is fuzzy and I feel like I'm looking at all of this through a long, dark tunnel. Suddenly, all I can hear is Tommy's words in my head…

RUN.

The guys are all yelling and talking at once. I push my hand against my lips to keep from screaming out and take off running as quickly as I can, looking for any potential place to hide. Heading into the cotton field, I hear one of them shout out.

"Where is the girl? Find her! We can't have any witnesses."

I push myself as hard as I can, but it doesn't take long for them to spot me. Suddenly, I hear multiple footsteps coming up behind me. I run as fast as I can, concentrating on not tripping. I'm not going to be one of those girls in a horror movie that falls only seconds before the monster catches her.

Unexpectedly, the sky lights up in front of me and I skid to a stop, blinded. My ears are ringing and there is an odd smell in the air. I reach my arms out, stepping forward slowly. Even though I can't see, I have to keep moving. I know those guys are only a few steps behind.

The sound of heavy footsteps has me stopping again because this time they seem like they are in front of me. Three large shapes appear in the outer field out of nowhere, a dim light encasing their massive forms. Something is wrong with the way they are standing. They look almost animalistic. My eyes slowly clear and I blink several times as I try to see through the sudden fog that seems to be surrounding us. They are still a good distance from me, but there is no denying they are something else.

Clicking noises and screeches reach my ears as they start sprinting toward me. I start to step back, only to turn and find myself only feet from the guys I had been running from in the first place. But they are no longer looking at me, they are focused on the things headed our way.

I immediately take advantage of their distraction and turn, running the opposite way across the field. I feel like I have only taken a few steps when I hear the guys start to scream. Pure terror has me running as fast as my legs will carry me. Something hitting me in the back knocks me to the ground. I scramble back to my feet, only to look down as I'm raising up. It's…a…head.

My mind doesn't even have time to comprehend what it's seeing as my next thoughts are interrupted when something sharp pierces my side. I start to fall, but before I can hit the ground, multiple hands grab me from behind and everything goes dark.

<h1 style="text-align:center">CHAPTER 3</h1>

I^{vy}

GENTLE HANDS STROKE MY FACE. "MOM," I whisper weakly. A damp cloth is laid across my eyes and as I reach up to remove it, someone touches my hand, stopping me.

Suddenly, something coming up in my throat gags me and I start coughing. I roll over onto my side and the rag falls off my face. I blink several times, but nothing looks familiar. Someone touching my arm has me looking up and even though I try to scream, only a shriek comes out. I start trembling all over the more I look around.

"Please be at ease. You are in no danger."

I scramble away until my back hits the wall behind me. My eyes dart around the room. There are several things… girls, something…and they are all looking at me. I must have either hit my head really hard or someone is playing one hell of a prank on me. Because if these girls are wearing outfits, they are way over the top. Their movements and coloring are unlike anything I have ever seen before. Looking at each one closely, I try to calm my breathing down. One of them has shimmering green scales, the other one seems to be covered in pink feathers, and her nose is pointed unnaturally. The other two are blue, but everything about their faces is wrong. Their bodies are un-proportioned, their arms seem to be too long, and it's like they have multiple elbows. There is no way a human could have manipulated their bodies to look like this.

They are talking among themselves. Have even pointed at me a few times, but their words don't make any sense. I shake my head, rubbing my eyes, hoping that when I open them back up…

This can't be real. My heart is beating out of my chest and tears run down my face freely. *Where in the hell am I?*

The one that is the closest to me stands up and I know my mouth is suddenly hanging open. Her skin shimmers in different shades of blue and it seems like she just keeps getting taller. There is no denying she is a female because she flaunts it freely, as she has done nothing to cover up her multiple breasts. There are gems and things placed upon her face and skin that make you focus on certain parts of her body, like the fact that her face is oblong. But the weirdest part is her cat-shaped green eyes. She stands above me, looking me up and down. I can tell I look just as odd to her as she does to me. She opens her mouth, saying something, but it takes a minute for me to understand her. "What are you?"

I'm shocked by her question and I immediately get defensive. "Me! Have you looked around?" I point at the others in the room.

"Yes, I am currently aware of my surroundings. You are a human. Is that correct?"

"Yea, where am I? What are you?"

She looks around at the others in the room and then back at me. "I'm Valerian and you are currently on Vormax. It's a pleasure center in the outer quadrant. You were delivered here a few rotations ago and put into our care."

I shake my head, then wipe the tears flowing down my face off angrily. "I'm sorry, but I'm really confused right now. You act as if I should know what or where that is. Look, it's apparent there has been a mistake in identities or something. I won't say a word. I'll tell people I had amnesia or something, but...I need to go home. I don't belong here. Who brought me here? Please! I just want to go home."

A sharp pain has me grabbing my head. I close my eyes tightly as the image of Tommy laying in the middle of the road with half his face gone hits me. Pieces of my life roll through my mind like a movie reel. The last one bothers me the most. Mom standing on the porch, watching me leave. I can hear her words plainly in my head as she warned me right before I left, *I will never see you again.*

I grab my head, pulling my knees up to my chest, and scream at the top of my lungs. *This isn't real,* I tell myself. *This is just a bad dream,* **this isn't real**. I keep thinking those words over and over. Suddenly, I feel a pinch on the side of my neck and I start to fall over. I lay there wide awake as they pull me from the bed, but I can't move a single muscle.

The thing, or girl, that was originally talking to me, picks me up effortlessly, my body limp in her arms as my head flops around. She lowers me into what feels like a warm jelly substance, and immediately it starts bubbling all around me. Multiple hands caress my hair and skin, gently cleaning me thoroughly. The more they talk, though, the more I'm beginning to understand the strange sounds they are making.

"Look at how delicate her limbs are. She won't make it long. Where do they find these fragile creatures, and why do they keep bringing them here just to perish so brutally? Their bodies nor their minds are equipped to handle our world."

"Unfortunately, she has already been selected. I tried to hide her arrival. I managed to get it entered onto the back of the list, but somehow they still got word of it. When the Master found out what she was, he decided to provide us with a higher security, but I could tell by the conversation we had earlier that he is at the point of disposing of her already due to the attention she is acquiring.

"If we had been able to keep her a secret for a few more risings, we may have been able to save her. The Qiznar who visited my quarters last darkness asked me if we have one of her kind in the house. He has always been kind, and I had no reason to deceive him, so I confirmed his questions about her. He informed me if I could contact Commander DaR, or even SoL, the reward they have on her kind would set several of us free, but it is too late to save this one. If we receive another, hopefully, we can hide her long enough to see if his words were accurate."

I listen half-heartedly, my mind still not comprehending that they are actually talking about me. They pass me around like a rag doll as they clothe me in a sheer fabric that flows all the way to my feet. The feathered one holds my head still while the other one fixes my hair and puts some kind of goop on my face. The tall blue one that has been talking this whole time kneels down in front of me. She is beautifully terrifying to look at. Her facial expressions and the intricate details on her skin are out of this world. I stop my random thoughts and focus on her. *Oh... my... God, she is real...they all are. They're aliens! That's what that light was in the field. ALIENS! It wasn't a nightmare. The guys in the truck,...they killed Tommy and then,...I really was knocked to the ground by someone's,... head.*

Her voice brings me back. "I am torn, little female, on whether to leave you like this or not. It is in your nature to fight back, but that will only get you damaged worse." She touches my face gently. "I need you to blink your eyes if you understand me."

I blink my eyes rapidly, pissed at the fact that I have no control over my body or my circumstances.

"There is not much we can do to prepare you, but you have every right to know what is going to happen. You have been purchased by an elite group of Waldrin. They rarely come to this planet as they are natural water dwellers and it is dry here. Unfortunately, though, for a few, they can still survive on land for short periods of time. The Master informed them that you cannot breathe underwater nor survive in their climate, and they have agreed to the restrictions put upon them.

"However, because of their demands and the outrageous price they paid for you, they have been given free rein to do with you as they please. The Master also had to provide them with a chamber made specifically to their specifications for the duration of their stay. Hopefully, the room will have adequate means for you to be able to survive, but I have no way of knowing for sure. The Waldrin are not a gentle race, and if provoked, well, they can become quite brutal, especially if they see you as substance. They also have multiple appendages that they will use to damage you all at once if they decide to. Also, they like to share their mates and what they consider food. I won't lie to you and tell you I believe you will survive them. Because I don't. I was hopeful when you were first brought to us that you had lived out the majority of your rotations, but it pains me to see that you are still so young.

"I have asked the Master multiple times to find another race for your introduction but the Waldrin were adamant about having you first. If I leave you like this, you will still feel everything, but your compliance may make your death quicker. If you fight them, it will become a sport to break you a little at a time and it will last much longer. Blink if you still understand me."

I blink, but this time tears flow down my cheeks when I do. She wipes them away and I can see that she is truly bothered by what is going to happen to me.

A booming voice enters the room, and she jerks away from me, standing quickly. She tries to block whoever comes in the room from me but is pushed roughly to the side. Something walks in front of me, but I can't raise my head up to see anything besides the dark brown robe it has on.

"You have wasted those coverings on her. Remove them immediately and wake her up. Our clientele has waited long enough."

I can see the blue girl wringing her hands together. Whoever this is, she is scared of. "Master, she is just a child. The clothing will at least give her some protection from their poisonous suckers."

He hesitates a moment before he answers her. "Very well, but you need to stop getting so attached to these temporary pets we receive. If she survives, we will heal her and then she will be sold. You will not see her or the likes of her again either way. I will not put our facility in any further danger for her kind. If the Korgons contact me again with one such as her, I'm going to inform them to dispose of them elsewhere. I'm no longer interested in them, even short-term. The credits are not worth the dangers they bring to our door. Now wake her up. I promised them a living creature, not a drugged corpse."

He no more walks off then I tumble out of my chair, gasping for breath as my knees hit the floor. The blue girl lifts me up until I'm standing on my feet. I try to yank away from her, but her hands grip me tightly.

She shakes me. "Stop fighting me and listen. The information I'm going to give you may be your only way to survive them. The Waldrin are at their weakest on land, even though it won't feel that way to you. Try your best not to get dragged into the water because they will drown you at the height of their feeding peak. There will be a point in that room that you will know there is no escaping them. No one has ever been able to escape their suckers once they have been latched onto. You need to find a place to go in your mind. A place to turn off the things that are happening to your body and simply let it happen. As long as they don't drown you, we can fix your physical body, but no one can fix a broken mind."

Tears flow down my face as I sob, pulling against her. "Please, please, just let me go. I want to go home. I want my mom… Please, just let me go." I'm practically screaming those last words.

"You no longer have a home to return to, youngling. This is your fate now." Red tears flow down her face as she pushes me into another's arms. "Take her. I can't bear to do it."

I scream and fight against the others as they pull me along effortlessly. A door is opened and I'm shoved through so roughly that I hit my knees. I scramble up, running back towards the doorway, only for it to be slammed in my face. I beat my fist against it, screaming for them to let me out. I turn around slowly, trying to see if there is any other way out of here. Taking a few steps forward, my toes sank into the powdery sand under my feet. The room looks like an expensive pool you would see in a catalog at a resort. The large body of water in front of me laps gently against the sand in small waves. For a moment, I let myself hope that the blue girl was wrong. I mean, surely nothing is hiding in all this beauty.

I scream, practically jump out of my skin when a high pitch shrill echoes off the walls. There are no words to describe the things that are suddenly rising up out of the water, sliding across the floor in front of me. I push back against the wall hard, sounds of denial coming out of my throat. *This isn't real, this isn't real… There is no such thing as monsters.*

I continue to watch in absolute horror as they just keep coming out of the water. Their brown flesh ripples from top to bottom. Repulsively, they look like worms,…worms with thousands of eyes placed all over their skin. *I hate fucking worms.* Different-length tentacles push them my way slowly as their long, rope-like appendages reach out from their sides, sliding them along the ground.

The biggest one in the front starts transforming into something else as it clears the water. Legs start stretching out of its mushy body and some of the tentacles that were pushing it out of the water start merging into multiple arms. The tentacles that still remain start moving like snakes as the body continues to change, all of them surrounded by large round suckers that pulse constantly, open and then close. Its body seems to solidify from what looks like mush to a hard shell the closer it gets to me. One of them reaches out. Alarmed, I duck out of its reach. "Keep your fucking suckers to yourselves, you ugly bastards!" I scream out.

It shrieks as I run the other way. I'm not stupid. The three of them are going to try and pin me. I scramble around the sand, ducking and running until I can barely breathe. At one point, I even try climbing the walls, but so far I have only managed to stay out of their reach as they hesitate to leave the edge of the water.

They finally stop moving, and it gives me a second to catch my breath. I mean, why do they want me? The last time I looked, humans and worms were not compatible. But wait a minute, didn't she say something about food? Hell's fucking fire, these bastards have been looking at me this whole time like I'm a rare steak in a fancy restaurant. They all turn back towards me at once, spreading out their arms, blocking me in. They have caught on that I can't get out of this room.

I missed one of the arms coming up behind me from the ground. The stinging sensation running up my leg has me falling to the ground, screaming. I crumble to the floor, as I can no longer bear any of my weight on that leg. I try to crawl away, screaming out when I see one of those long, fingerless arms coming my way, but there is nowhere left for me to go.

Suddenly, I'm surrounded by all three of them. Multiple arms grab me all at once. I fight against them as the clothes I was dressed in are quickly torn away. Their tentacles surround my whole body in a wiggling, blanket-like mass attaching themselves to my most sensitive parts. Just as I thought it couldn't get any worse, they start injecting me with thousands of burning needles all at once.

The sound that leaves my throat echoes off the walls as they laugh and screech around me. The electrical shocks they are sending into my body overwhelm my senses, leaving me barely holding onto consciousness. I twitch and spasm as their suckers move all over my skin. There isn't a piece of my skin that is not being subjected to the poison in their needles they are shoving into me.

I have been pulled right up against one of them and the way its skin pulses and folds. I feel like I'm being absorbed as I feel a burning secretion start covering my stomach and legs. Multiple small tentacles trace every inch of me, including inside my ears and nose. One even raises my eyelid, rubbing my eye before it moves on.

No amount of warning could have prepared me for such horrors or the pain… How do you turn such agony off? I try to push it away, but it's become all-consuming. They told me to think of something else. At this point, I can no longer think or concentrate on anything,… but the pain. How do you prepare anyone for this type of constant torture? They screech and scream in delight as my body goes limp. I'm being held in such a way that I'm no longer in control of anything, nor do I have the strength left to fight, as these gross and disgusting things explore me at will.

Dark spots form in front of my eyes and I can feel my thoughts slipping away as I plead for death, anything to make this indescribable nightmare stop. The things stop moving around me suddenly, and for a split second, I pray they have tired of me.

But my prayers are not answered and all at once they're everywhere inside of me. My nose, mouth, ears, vagina, and butt are invaded all at once. Just when I thought that was going to be the worst of it, the suckers on their arms start boring into my skin. I don't even have the energy left to try and scream as my body can no longer feel the differences in all this agony as it's all become the same now.

I start convulsing as my body is being smothered by the things that have invaded my nose and throat. It rams itself into me hard everywhere at once and I gag on the tentacle down my throat. My skin is being peeled slowly from my muscles as it sucks me in tighter. They are squeezing me so tightly that it feels like my bones are being snapped slowly. Being smashed is more than my mind can handle, and I let the pain, the helplessness take my consciousness to a place of silence. The last thing that flashes through my mind… is Mom. She was right all along. *They literally are going to chew me up and spit me out.*

CHAPTER 4

A vX

I WALK OUT onto the training field behind our main family home and up to XuL as he watches the young ones.

"Good rising, brother. I see they have you up early."

"This rising, Zura has decided to bring one of the younger females to work with Keida. She wants to see her skill level before Father and her decide where to start her training."

"I feel like our little Keida grows taller every time I see her."

"Both younglings are aging quicker than I like. I was completely against this training until lately and their confrontation with SiN.

I would prefer to keep her young and innocent as long as possible, but life seems to be fighting me in that area. What brings you here this rising, AvX?"

"SoL wanted me to sit in on an interrogation. Once I was finished, I figured I would come to see my girl. Her birthday is coming up and I need to get a head start on the others looking for something for her."

"Brit and I have given up on such things. With all of you buying her whatever she wants, there is nothing left for us to get. See that new sword she just walked out with? She recently conned SoL into getting that little jewel for her. She should be home playing with her dolls and enjoying the innocence of her youth instead of all this violence. I almost took the sword from her, but she was adamant about wanting one of her own. Especially since Danny has one, but he is older and even though I shouldn't think this way, he is a male. I feel differently about him having one. She is my baby and I pray she doesn't get injured too badly with it."

We both get quiet when the bell is rung for everyone to meet in the center of the field. I hadn't been paying any attention to anyone but Keida up to this point, but now I can see that several younglings are gathering in the middle. Zura's immense height stands out severely above the others as they gather around her.

She starts pairing the children up, giving them all instructions as they head off to other parts of the field. It's not long before the only ones left near her are Keida and Danny.

Zura waves someone else onto the field. Another female enters, taking her cloak off, revealing her warrior clothing underneath. This girl is only a few Orbital rotations older than Danny and she is starting to fill out. He doesn't hide his reaction to her young beauty before Keida catches him standing there with his mouth practically open. She looks down at her own outfit of a cute pair of pink shorts and what Brit calls a tank top, then back at the girl.

From here, I can feel her instant anger and sudden determination. XuL and I walk closer so that we can hear Zura's instructions, but not close enough to interfere.

"Keida, this is Zvranna. You two will be doing quite a bit of training together for the next few rotations. This rising we are going to go through a few simple maneuvers until I can see what your weaknesses and strengths are. Remember, these swords in your hands are not toys and you can do some real damage to the other person if not careful. However, with that being said, I do not want to see either of you holding back either."

Keida points toward the girl. "Why is she dressed like that? I was not given any other clothing to appear in."

"Zvranna has passed two warrior trials, and that is when all our females are given their first battle garments. She is required to dress according to her station from this point on. You will be granted the same as you advance, but because of your status, you will not be required to dress the same."

Zura steps back and motions for the girls to advance on each other. Danny stands off to the side, his hand on Keida's big Selin,

SeeSee. The animal snarls every time the girl swings her sword, connecting with Keida's. Raven walks the perimeter all around them, her bright blue eyes never missing a thing.

Zvranna swings hard at Keida, and she almost loses her footing as she slides backward. I hear a massive growl leave SeeSee and XuL starts to head into the ring until I put my hand out to stop him. The father in him immediately wants to stop this before his baby gets hurt.

"Wait, she is fine. Keida was simply letting her think she was getting the best of her. Watch!" Within the next couple of swings, the other girl is on the defense as Keida steadily pushes her backward. With a twist of her wrist, Keida disarms the girl, and she is flat on her back with her hands up, trying to defend herself, Keida's sword pushed into her neck.

Keida backs away, never taking her eye off the other girl as she does. She bends down and picks up the other girl's sword, expertly swinging both of them in her hands, a small smirk on her face as she looks up at Zura. "I would prefer to train with both swords from now on if that's ok with you."

Zura puts her hand out, helping the younger girl up, then turns back to Keida. "I will say I'm impressed and shocked. I owe you an apology, as I was judging you by your small stature. I will not underestimate you again. You demonstrated the strength and skills to proceed in any direction you prefer. I will discuss your further training with General XuL and Commander Dar. We will commence next rising, same time."

Keida nods and then turns toward Danny, who has been watching all of this quietly from the side. She raises her sword up, pointing it at him. "I didn't and don't appreciate the way you are looking at her. If it happens again or continues, you will be sleeping in your own room from this point on."

I have to turn around to keep from laughing. Danny's face turns red, but before he can say anything back, Zura yells out his name, and it's his turn to spar with some of the other males. Keida watches him walk off, making sure he doesn't glance over at the other girl before she launches herself up onto SeeSee's back. The large animal shakes his head, agitated as they walk off the field together.

Everyone who came to watch the younglings steps back and out of the way as they walk past. Not only are they terrified of the Selin, but I feel a few of them looking at Keida with new respect. They all underestimated her because of how protective her family is, they expected her to be spoiled and uncooperative. She proved this rising, that she is more than just a pretty face or even someone's daughter or granddaughter. She is a warrior in a pretty and deceiving package.

She spots us up on the hill and nudges SeeSee towards us. Her long brown, pink, and white hair flies out behind her as they ride swiftly toward us. She launches herself off his back as soon as she is within my reach. I catch her midair, laughing at her carefree spirit, enjoying the feeling of her complete love and the confidence she has in me catching her.

She squeezes my neck tightly before kissing me on the cheek. "Unka AvX, I haven't seen you in forever. You haven't forgotten my birthday, have you?"

"Oh, how you wound me. How could I ever forget my favorite girl?"

She stops for a second, her pink eyes twirling mesmerizing in front of me. "I won't always be your favorite, but that's ok. It seems to happen to all grownups sooner or later."

"You will always be my best girl. There is no other who has captured my heart as you have. I was very proud of you out there today."

She pulls my head over so that she can whisper in my ear. "Thank you, I have been training bunches in the simulator on Falcor. Unka Tordy is going to help Daddy install one in the main house for me for my birthday. They don't think I know anything about it."

I kiss her cheek and whisper back. "It's our secret. Now, speaking of your big day. How old are you going to be, sixteen?"

She rolls her eyes at me. "No, Unka AvX, I'll be eight."

"What happened to seven?"

"That's what I am now. You didn't miss it."

"You need to stop getting older. It's making me feel ancient. What do you want for your birthday?"

She shrugs her shoulders. "I don't know." I feel sadness from her for a second before she looks past me and back out on the field where Danny is fighting a couple of boys at one time. He may be smaller than the surrounding others, but he is more confident in his skills. He swings his sword, poised for the next attack. I can feel that Zura is impressed with both children. I just hate that they are both having to learn to defend themselves. These should be the best years of their lives, full of fun and play.

Keida lets out a small whistle that makes my ears ring and Raven turns our way and away from Danny. She gallops up the hill, brushing along SeeSee's side right before she stops in front of me. Raven is a massive animal. She is so tall; the top of her head is barely a few inches shorter than my own. She nudges Keida's leg affectionately before she turns back towards Danny.

"Why did you call her away?"

"He is going to get nicked here in a minute, and she gets really upset when he gets hurt. I wasn't down there to keep her from attacking the boy who is going to do it, and she would have gone after him without one of us there to stop her."

She no more says this than Danny grabs his side. His hands flare out an odd blue aura, but this is the only sign he gives off that he is injured as he continues to fight back. Raven growls and starts to step forward, only for a click of Keida's tongue stops her.

"Let me down. She won't stay here as soon as she smells his blood." Keida walks under Raven's neck, talking to her soothingly before they both start walking back toward the field. SeeSee turns, following right behind them. Keida stops looking back at me for a second. "Unka AvX, don't worry about being late. I'll be eight for a while. Love you, and trust your feelings even when you think they are not there."

I watch her walk away, and for the first time, I'm worried about her future. "XuL, how do you do it?"

"What?"

"Not lock her up in a safe room where nothing can ever damage her love or trust."

"It has taken me many sleepless nights to come to terms with her afflictions. Every father wishes to protect their child, and honestly, it's a nonstop struggle not to grab her and Brit and run far away. I know in my heart, though, there is no other place she could be safer.

"Even if she didn't have me, my brothers, father, or even her grandfather, those two animals would give their lives to save hers and let's not forget Danny. He is becoming a warrior with unparalleled powers. He is the one we should all pity because he gets her anger and her pain, while we only get her love. There are times I wish I could see what their future holds. Because even a blind man can see the ties that link them together. You know, SoL is a few points ahead of you with that new sword of hers. If you're going to keep up the favorite Unka title, you are going to have to up your game."

"It's been on my mind for a few rotations now. I can't let the big guy win with a simple sword. I have some shopping to do. I'll return before her birthday."

He grabs my arm, pulling me close as he pats me on the back. "Safe travels, brother."

I look back at Keida once more and then start towards my personal shuttle. Once I am airborne. "Falcor, can you put me through to ANDI?"

"Confirmed."

ANDI's cheerful voice comes across the speakers. "Master AvX, what do I owe the pleasure?"

"Do you have anything on your flight log for the next few rotations? I'm in need of a special present for our Keida and could use your assistance as I'm going planet hopping."

"My logs are empty because of the upcoming solar storms that are being predicted in the area, but the Traveler is a tough old girl and she can take it. Don't let Falcor know this, but I'm bored and ready to head out."

Falcor butts in, "ANDI, I can hear your every communication."

I shake my head, laughing. "ANDI, get fired up. I'll be headed your way once I leave the planet's atmosphere."

CHAPTER 5

A vX

"ANDI, I never dreamed it would be this hard to find a small child a present. I can't believe after all this we have still found nothing. I'm worn out. It feels like I have walked across the outer quadrants one planet at a time."

"AvX, this was your seventh market. I have mentioned this before, but if you could give me an idea of what you're looking for. I might be able to help."

"Up to this point, I was hoping something would simply jump out at me when I saw it. She is easily pleased, but the older she gets, the more complicated this is getting. I'm looking for something unique, an item no one else could provide for her. She loves animals. If I could find something that SeeSee or Raven wouldn't eat, that would be perfect, but I feel like the odds are against me."

"AvX, what about a bird of some sort? They were commonly kept as pets on Earth. They had thousands of different species on that planet. It is so sad that they were all lost so brutally."

"ANDI, you have mentioned Earth several times on our quest for the ultimate present. Do you miss it?"

"I miss its uniqueness. It was a world forgotten, still primitive in many ways, and advanced in others. To be able to witness their growths and advancements was amazing, though. TY and I had a lot of hardships there, as you know, but the good times were just as rewarding. I will put some feelers out and see if we might be able to find an exotic or rare animal sale at one of the upcoming markets."

"I leave the controls and our heading in your capable hands, ANDI. I'm drained and in need of a long nap. Once I awaken, if you have not uncovered anything by then, I'll help with the search."

I was turning away from the helm when a bright light flashes across the main viewer and the ship vibrates lightly. "ANDI, that one was overly bright. Should we dock somewhere for a few risings until the flares pass?"

"We are currently flying out of their projected flight pattern. Within half a rising, we will be out of their range altogether. Unfortunately, we may have to reassess our path on our return."

My head no sooner hits the pillow than I fall into a deep sleep. This is something I rarely get to experience, as my mind is always picking up the feelings of others near me. My male Valerian heritage exposes my mind to other's powerful emotions or moods. I have learned to block them when I'm awake, but when sleep comes. I frequently find myself living through another's views. The silence is a welcome change and also just as startling when ANDI blurts my name. I jerk straight up, momentarily unaware of my surroundings.

"AvX, we are approaching the next market and I believe this one may have a few unique items available. They have several vendors that specialize in the personalization of weapons and jewelry. What female doesn't like those things? I have already arranged docking and your shuttle is fueled and ready when you are."

I roll my neck, then rub my hands through my hair, feeling out of sorts this rising. Maybe the quiet is messing with me, as I'm not used to being in my own head alone. "Thank you, ANDI. I will be there shortly." I dress quickly, then head towards the shuttle bay.

ANDI's voice comes over the speakers when I enter the room. "I have already programmed your shuttle with your landing coordinates. Happy shopping. I hope you find the one thing you have been searching for all this time."

"Me too. Next Orbital, I'm sending her credits so she can go get whatever she wants. I'm too old to chase the stars looking for the impossible." The trip planetside is uneventful. Unfortunately, the moment I lower the ramp, multiple thoughts bombard me. I immediately shove them away and focus on finding my way to their primary market.

Dreading the crowd of the market and distracted, I almost miss a small Valerian male approaching me hesitantly. "Pardon me, but are you one of Commander DaR's, sons?"

"I am. My name is AvX. Can I be of service?"

"I knew when I was told of your shuttle landing, all would be well." He starts wringing his hands together, and I can tell he is overly nervous because his thoughts are all over the place. "Excuse my bad manners. I am known as Vance. I'm a cargo box trader here on Marin and I have something that may interest you. If you would come with me, it is just a short distance to my main warehouse."

"I'm not the one you need to speak to if you want to discuss trades for your merchandise. I'm here on a personal errand, but I can put you in contact with the right person."

"Unfortunately, that is not what I need your help with, even though that would have likely been easier to deal with. I understand you have no reason to accompany me, but I desperately need your assistance with something that I believe comes from your father's primary planet."

I motion for him to lead the way, notifying ANDI of my location before I enter the darkened building. There are crates and boxes piled up everywhere. I let my senses stretch out, only detecting myself and the other male inside. We only walk a short distance before he pauses in front of a cage. Pointing at the large female AllTarra sitting on top of it.

I'm shocked. "How did she come to be here? Their kind is protected across the universe because of their rarity. Who would be foolish enough to capture and try to sell one of their kind, especially at a market? Everyone knows there is only a handful left within the dark forest on Darverius." I'm truly puzzled by her appearance here. "How did they get past the Selin to even retrieve her? Father will need to be contacted immediately."

He shakes his head yes. " I had those same thoughts the moment I opened her crate. Immediately, I sent out a notice to your father, but it was returned to me unopened. I have tried several other methods to get a hold of him. Especially when I opened the bottom cage, but I was told the solar flares were messing up most of the correspondence coming in and out."

"Who did you purchase her from?"

"As much as I would love to tell you that, I have no way of knowing who the original owner was. I purchase random merchandise from a cloaked dealer. The ones who brought them here are contracted out to make the deliveries. Normally, they do not know what is even in the containers. And until this shipment, everything I have received up to this point has been simply an overabundance of every-rising items like soaps, brushes, and so forth. I mark the items cheap and sell them to the poorer citizens in our area, or simply donate the entire crates to local charities.

"As you can see around here, most of the things are delivered sealed up in crates. I had no idea there was even anything alive at first until I heard the AllTarra shrieking through one of the enclosures. I was as shocked as you are now when I first opened it up. However, she is not the only reason I brought you here. You see, there is something I believe is even more rare in the cage beneath her. But watch out before you step forward. The AllTarra is very protective of the creature and she won't let me get too close."

I start to walk forward only for the AllTarra to flare her massive wings, stopping me from getting any closer. I hold still, refusing to back away. As I project my feelings toward her, she takes a few steps back. I can feel her distrust of me, as she has been handled roughly. One of her wings hangs low, and it's causing her quite a bit of discomfort. I try asking her if this male was the cause of her injury, but all she can show me are shadows and someone in a mask.

Speaking softly, I tell her, "I'm only going to look inside. I won't touch it." At first, I think she is going to refuse me, but she backs away from the front of the cage slowly. I kneel down and it takes me a second for my eyes to focus on the shape in the back of the darkened cage.

Rage, unlike anything I have ever felt before, flares through me, and my runes brighten as my muscles bulk under my anger. I turn, grabbing the male by his neck, holding him high up in the air.

"I should snap your neck here and now. Explain yourself!"

He grabs at my hands, trying to free himself. I sort through his feelings quickly, the fact that he expected me to react this way has me lowering him back to the ground, but I don't release him from my grasp.

"Please let me explain. I have tried to get her out of that cage several times. I even had a healer come once, but every time someone touches her, her screams of agony are unbearable to listen to. The healer told me that someone had half-healed her and dumped her in that cage to die. You can see the clothing and blankets I put in there with her still laying in the corner of the cage. She has refused to use them. It took me a few risings to understand that she can't bear anything touching her skin. Once I figured that out, I had the crate lifted off the floor. Then I turned the heat up in here as much as possible, but she is slowly fading away.

"The AllTarra has bonded to her and has been feeding her almost like she is one of her chicks. The bird is all that has kept her alive these last risings. She has been literally forcing the nutrients into her mouth. This is the only thing that has kept her from fading away. I have done everything in my power to get her to eat or drink, only to fail. You have to take them both from here. I know you have the means to heal her body, but I hope that you can also heal her mind. As I said, I was trying my best to get hold of your father. I have no knowledge of what she is, but there have been rumors of the Commander mating with an off-worlder, and there is no denying she is unknown."

I take my hands off him, and slowly he steps back from me, out of reach, rubbing his neck. "You are extremely large to be one of us. Valerians are not known to be warriors, but caretakers."

"I can thank my father for my enhanced size." I walk around the enclosure, but the female never moves, or even acknowledges that I'm there. That's when it hits me. Nothing, I feel nothing from her. How is that possible?

"I will have to contact my ship. I need to figure out the best way to transport her and the AllTarra without injuring either of them worse. The ship I'm traveling on has a med chamber, but I'm not sure we are equipped to handle this. Has she ever responded, or is it only when being touched?"

"No responses at all. It hurts my heart that I have not been able to provide better for her. No female should be treated like this, but I was scared to force her out of the cage and damage her more. When she does open her eyes, it's like there is nothing behind them. Her pupils don't even move if you wave your hand in front of her.

"As you can see, the poor thing is filthy, but I dare not try to clean her up. When I first opened the container, she was covered in some sort of parasite, but the AllTarra picked them off her skin one darkness. After that, I left the cage open, hoping she would crawl out on her own.

"I have left the front door open like this ever since. The AllTarra at least provides some warmth for her. She never touches her with her wings, but she flares them out above her when darkness comes. She does seem to relax some from the warmth. I will assist you in any way to get her to your ship and pray to the Lord of Light that you can heal her tortured soul, for I fear her mind is broken."

I touch my personal comm unit on my wrist. "ANDI, can the shuttle be re-conformed to fit a container this size, or do I need to hire a transport?"

"Hold your communicator towards the object and I will be able to assess it better. Oh, this is concerning. I can recalibrate the loading area in the shuttle, but the AllTarra will be a problem if not contained properly. They don't travel well."

I turn back towards Vance. "Do you think she would hurt the female if I put her in the same cage?"

"The AllTarra has been remarkably gentle with her. So no, I don't believe she would hurt her intentionally."

"ANDI?"

"Give me a few minutes and I will have the shuttle finished. We need to get both of them on board as quickly as possible. The AllTarra is young and needs to be healed before her wing is damaged permanently, as well as the human female."

I project the feeling of safety and home toward the AllTarra hoping she understands what I'm trying to do. I don't know who is more shocked, me or Vance, when she tucks her wings in and simply walks into the cage standing in front of the female.

Closing the door, I click the lock in place. "Do you have a lift I can borrow to get them to the shuttle?"

"Let me go retrieve it."

CHAPTER 6

A vX

VANCE WASN'T LYING about the screams. I almost jumped out of my skin the first time she did it. We managed to lift the crate up without moving her around, but when we went to put it on the hover lift, it bumped the door before steadying the load, causing her body to rock back and forth, commencing a sound that will haunt my dreams.

Immediately, I ran around to the side closest to her face, trying to calm her, only to once again feel nothing from her. She isn't even projecting the pain she is feeling outward. It's like the screams are reactional. I have never felt so helpless, or like such a monster. There is no other way for me to get her on board and if this is jarring her around too much. I can't imagine what the shuttle is going to do.

She whimpers as Vance starts easing her forward, and we both stop. "I'm sorry AvX, but this female is ripping my old heart out with those screams of hers. I feel her pain like it's my own with every step."

"You can actually feel her?"

"Not in the same sense you can and, up to this point, I was hesitant about giving her any medications, but we have to do something."

"ANDI, can you contact SAGE and see if we can safely sedate her? I'm not going to be able to move her like this."

"The solar flares are making communications difficult, but let me look into something fast. After all, SAGE gets the majority of her information from my old logs of Earth."

There is silence for a few minutes.

"AvX, I have the chemicals available on board to lightly sedate her. Unfortunately, I have not been able to locate what is needed on Marin. Human bodies are extremely fragile, especially when damaged. Her best odds are for you to get her here as quickly as possible, even if it causes her more discomfort."

"In other words, you are telling me to let her scream. I don't know if I'm capable of doing that, ANDI."

"I'm scanning every scenario through my databases now and none of them are coming up with the answers we are both seeking. The trip from the planet only takes a few moments. If the pain is as severe as you say, her screams will end shortly after takeoff. Her body will shut down naturally."

"Lord of Light, forgive me for what I'm about to do," I whisper to myself.

I hit the controls on the hover lift before I change my mind and I start moving her forward. Telling myself the whole time that the faster I can get her to ANDI, the quicker we can take this pain from her. The AllTarra pecks at me if the female whimpers, but for the most part she simply watches us as we move her from the warehouse to the shuttle. I open the cargo hold, grateful that ANDI rearranged it so that the crate could fit in securely.

Vance looks up at me when he sees me hesitating to lift the crate in manually. "Take the hover lift. It may help keep her steady in the air. I will purchase another one later."

"That's an excellent idea. Here, let me transfer some credits to your account to help offset that expense. These things are not cheap."

He backs away from me, shaking his head no. "Taking her screams is payment enough. The only thing I ask. If it's not too much trouble, could you please send me a communication later on, telling me if she survived?"

"I will send it personally."

"Until then." He nods respectfully at me, looks at the girl once more, and then walks away.

I move the whole thing into the shuttle and then squeeze past it to my seat. I hit the button for the ramp to close. The crate sits snugly against the door, and I flinch when it rocks slightly as the cabin pressurizes. I take a deep breath and initiate the launch sequence.

I have always enjoyed flying and up until this very moment I have paid little attention to the forces of lift-off. The shuttle hovers momentarily above the ground, then launches upward. A small whimper has me turning, looking back toward the crate. I should have known that wouldn't be the worst of it. The second we break through the atmosphere, the shuttle jerks. The scream that comes from behind me has me holding my ears.

It only lasts a second, but it feels like a lifetime. The moment the shuttle lands in the docking bay, I practically fall out of it trying to escape the horror of the sounds coming out of her.

The AllTarra is squawking and pecking at the bars aggressively, but the female has fallen quiet once again.

"ANDI?"

"I'm preparing the medical chamber as we speak. AvX, I know you are feeling like you are failing her, but considering the circumstances, you have done great. Just concentrate on the fact that we are only moments from making her comfortable.

However, your job is not finished yet. You still have to get her there."

I walk back to the shuttle, sending calming waves toward the AllTarra. She settles down reluctantly, but she is still not happy.

Unwillingly, I start the process of unloading the crate. It would have been so much faster if I could have picked her up and taken her to medical. With that sudden thought, I still have no idea how to get her out of this cage once I get her there.

She doesn't make another sound as I remove the crate from the shuttle. The hover lift adjusts to the floor of the ship effortlessly and I push it gently toward the main ship. There are a few places I have to maneuver it several ways to get it down the corridor, but I finally get her to the med bay. I'm a wreck by the time I do, my nerves stretched tightly.

"You did well, AvX, now let's get the AllTarra out first."

I open the door on guard and prepare for the large bird's attack. Shockingly, she walks up to the open door, making small cooing noises. I hold out my hand, projecting healing and safety her way. When she hops up into my hand, I'm happily shocked. I raise her up slowly and place her on a perch that ANDI had constructed while we were transporting them here.

She hops off my hand and over to the perch, little growly noises rattle her frame as she settles on it comfortably. I start to turn away from her when she reaches out with one of her long claws, pulling my hand back. I stiffen up, expecting her to strike out at me, but she lowers her beak down close to my hand, depositing something shiny into it.

She straightens back up and then looks me right in the eye. Then towards the female still in the cage. I lift my hand up, trying to figure out where she got what appears to be little hairs in my palm.

I rub my finger over one of them and it sticks me sharply. "ANDI, what did she just put in my hand?"

"Insert them under my scanner and I will process them while you get the girl out of the cage."

I flick them into the tray that just came out of the wall, while rubbing the discomfort in my palm where one of them stung me. The AllTarra screeches loudly, suddenly agitated as I start to bend down and crawl into the cage. Her wings flash brightly as she stretches them out, even with one of them still hanging lower than the other.

"AvX, hold your breath until I tell you it's safe." I feel a mist of cold air surround me and then the AllTarra calms. She tucks her head under her uninjured wing, relaxing into what looks like a peaceful sleep. Small mechanical arms come out of the wall, beginning to work on her injury.

"You can breathe now. I have cleared the chamber of the suppressant. The medical chamber will reset her wing and she will sleep peacefully until it heals."

I turn back to the female still in the cage, dreading trying to get her out of it. "ANDI, any suggestions?"

"Yes, we are going to do this a little differently than we did the AllTarra. Close your eyes and hold your breath, then count to ten. This will give me time to numb her body momentarily."

I feel the mist settle on me once again, this time my own skin numbs lightly anywhere the mist touches me.

"Ok, get her out as quickly as possible."

"How?"

"I don't know, but try to touch her as little as possible."

I crawl inside, looking at her slight frame. I grab one wrist and then an ankle, lifting her off the floor a few inches before quickly squirming my way back out. I was lifting her above the bed, ready to lay her down upon it, when ANDI's voice stops me.

"Don't lay her down! Hold her above the bed until the medical chamber can calibrate her weight. You will know when to let go."

Suddenly, she is lifted away from me, and her body starts to hover above the bed. Invisible hands straighten her out on her back as different colored beams of light start passing back and forth over her body. When one of the beams crosses over one of her long legs, I notice something shimmering on her legs.

"ANDI, are you seeing these shiny things along her legs?"

"Yes, I'm trying to determine their originality. I believe this is what is causing all her pain. I have scanned the ones that AllTarra showed you and they match the ones on the human female. She must have been trying to show you what was wrong with the girl; and they say animals are stupid. Whoever said that, apparently, has never been around any of ours. Anyway, those things are not just on her legs. If my scanners are accurate, there isn't a single pore on her skin not infected with one of these. Something deliberately did this to her.

"I contacted SCOUT and have forwarded the information to him and SAGE. SCOUT's processors are quicker than mine and he will be able to give us some direction on how to move forward with her.

"I do have some good news, though. The female has entered into the early stages of malnutrition. This means her body still retains the resources to help us fight the things that have been implanted into her skin. She is small, but no more than any of the other human females I'm acquainted with. From the bone scans I have received, she must have been very young when taken. Her muscles and organs have the familiar marks of stasis, but her youth has kept them from breaking down."

"ANDI, can you clean her up some? I can't tell if something is an injury or dirt."

"I'm scared to use anything at this time, at least until SCOUT can get back with me. Wait a minute, he is hailing me now. Go ahead, SCOUT. I'll put you on the speaker."

"Master AvX, ANDI, we may lose this transmission shortly, so listen up. The female has been injected with Waldrin needles. Waldrin's use these needles to absorb nutrients from their prey straight into their soft, fleshy bodies. They go into a euphoria-type trance once they start feeding. Pain and fear are both like drugs for them. The pain is unexplainable and unfortunately, not many survive once caught within their tentacles. The agony this female was subjected to while these needles were being inserted can't even be measured. It's not shocking she's unresponsive right now.

"My processor is still analyzing a way to treat her, but when I first started researching the sample ANDI sent to me. An interesting problem was brought to my attention that will have to be dealt with immediately. Because I won't have time to go into every-thing, I have initiated an alternate course for the Traveler to follow until I can get a better idea of how bad the situation is, and she has already left the port of Marin. I didn't mean to over-ride your command, ANDI, but word is out that the female was in Marin. I knew you had all sensors focused on her at this time, and would have not been prepared for an ambush.

"Master AvX, it looks like you just brought on board a criminal. This Human female has an immense bounty on her head. It's being said that she single-handedly killed three Waldrin of elite status from the evidence I have been able to collect. They were in the process of absorbing her when suddenly their bodies started increasing in heat rapidly and then breaking out with huge blisters.

"Before they could pull their needles out of her skin, they started shriveling up. Because of their water-dwelling nature, their bodies have to remain cool and wet. The fevers that overtook their forms would have led to a horrendously excruciating death for all involved. Apparently, something in her blood attacked their system, killing them within moments of them starting to feed from her. I'm simply assuming this part of the story, as I still don't have all the facts, but I would say they were at a pleasure center. The place would have had to report the deaths of the Waldrin to the authorities because of their status. But they also knew Human females were illegal to trade, which was going to reflect badly on their business. So, they healed her enough to ship her off their planet. I can't stress to you how low the odds were of you finding her.

"When I originally looked at her scans, I couldn't process how many of these needles they had inserted, but now the number has been revealed, I must urge you to act quickly. They have to be removed immediately because every time she is stung, by one of them moving it's slowly killing her. They are still operating as if still connected to their host. They are absorbing the nutrients in her skin and body rapidly. The problem is how to remove them without permanently destroying her skin. Hold please."

SAGE's holo form appears on the foot of the bed, but her form is waving in and out of focus.

SCOUT's angry voice echoes throughout the room. "SAGE! Return to your main processor immediately. If you get disconnected mid-connection, you will be permanently erased."

"I know the risk, SCOUT, but I couldn't help without being able to see her. I don't have time to argue about this. AvX, I have approximately thirty seconds to tell you how to treat her before a solar flare disrupts this transmission. Her skin needs to be peeled. There is a thick, honey-like textured chemical I'm sending to ANDI for him to make for you to put on her skin. You have to apply it, let it dry, then peel it off slowly. The cream will be painful to remove, so try to keep her under as much as possible. The ones inside of her body you will have to burn out. ANDI will have to oversee that himself, as the procedure could damage her tender skin permanently. Also, before I forget... where she has been laying on her side, those needles will be deep. Once you remove what you can with the cream, any that remain, you will have to remove manually. This is going to be a long, tedious procedure."

SCOUT yells out. **"SAGE, three seconds!"** And I swear I feel his emotions so strong in my head that my knees almost buckle.

SAGE disappears before she can tell us anything else. The Traveler shakes under my feet and the lights flicker a few times. "ANDI?"

"I'm a little busy here, AvX!"

"Did something just hit us?"

"Busy!"

The room starts to tilt, and I grab onto the bed. I start to reach for the girl, only to find that she is still safely hovering above everything. The ship vibrates violently for what feels like forever before it suddenly settles down.

"Sorry about that, AvX, but that last flare knocked us around a bit. I'm going to have to repair one of the outer hull plates quickly. I barely got us out of range before it burned a hole clear through us."

"I'm not comfortable with us landing somewhere public, especially now with what SCOUT told us about the female."

"Do you trust me?"

"You do have my life in your hands, so I would assume that's a yes, ANDI."

"There are some rogue asteroids in our path and I'm going to land on the back side of one of them until this storm passes."

"You can do that?"

"Ye, of little faith, of course, I can, in theory."

"How long until you can prove if your theory will be effective?"

"Well…hold on until I tell you not to."

CHAPTER 7

A vX

THE SHIP TILTS SUDDENLY, and I hit the side of the table hard. "Frack, ANDI you're beating us to death back here."

"I told you to hold on. I wasn't saying that to hear my own voice."

The ship's thrusters suddenly start to decrease in power, and we land roughly on something. "I really hope we just landed on your intended target."

"We have landed safely, and at the moment, we are fully cloaked. Falcor and SCOUT are the only two with the coordinates of our current location. You are rubbing your arm. Do you need medical attention?"

"No, I'm good. Someone's crazy ass flying knocked me into the table."

"I will let that slur slide, as I know my navigational skills are well above average. We have wasted enough time. Let's get started on the female. I'm eager to get these abominations out of her skin. I have prepared the concoction that SAGE sent me. I felt like a medicine man from earth mixing so many organic herbs together. I hope we will have her up and about quickly once these have been removed."

A large bowl suddenly appears out from the side of the bed, a thick, gooey substance inside. "How are we supposed to apply this? It's not like I can rub this on her skin without doing more damage."

"I'll have a dropper for you momentarily. I perceived that was going to be an issue as I was mixing it. It should be large enough that you can control the amount being applied without actually touching her skin."

I take a moment to look over her slight frame. She is covered in dirt and has small but very visible injuries all over her. "Lord of Light, I don't know where to start."

"Start at her shoulder and work your way down the arm. Once we have the medicine applied, it has to set for a few minutes before it hardens. As it's doing that, you can move on to other parts of her body. This process is going to be very time-consuming, and I don't know if we can even finish in one rotation."

"How do we get it back off once it hardens?"

"It will have to be peeled slowly from her skin. I'm going to keep her sedated, because the removal of the needles may be as painful coming out as they were going in. I know her species is new to you, but all humans have small, almost invisible hairs all over their bodies and this medication is going to rip everything out. That alone would be painful."

"Won't this destroy her skin in the process?"

"SAGE's last report said that her skin would turn red and that she would need healing baths, possibly a few times afterward. AvX, you will have to be my hands for this procedure as I can't physically touch the female and some of the things we will need to do to heal her properly will most likely make you very uncomfortable."

"I'm already uncomfortable, ANDI. I wish we could have flown her straight back to Darverius, where they have healers and the medical chambers available to fix all of these injuries."

"In a perfect world that would have been nice, but we would have had to treat the female either way, as we are rotations away from the care she needs immediately. For once, our miracle medical chamber would not have been able to help with this affliction. It was designed to piece humans back together, not take things out. Now, quit stalling, and let's get to it."

I lift the bowl up and the applicator, then slowly drip a small amount onto her shoulder. The paste smells odd, but not unpleasant. It takes me a few tries to get the amount correct, but once I get the thickness right, it starts to harden. As the hardening progresses, the needles become clearer as they start to turn black. The cream pulls them up effortlessly as her skin reacts to the chemicals in the mix.

I wait patiently until ANDI tells me to start peeling it off. Then, trying to be as gentle as possible, I lift a small piece on the top of her shoulder slowly. It peels away effortlessly, lifting hundreds of needles out in the process. I manage to peel her entire arm at once, only stopping the process when I get to the crease of her hand.

"ANDI, should we continue with the cream or stop and make sure they are all out in sections?"

"Let me scan the area you just did and we will see if any remain."

I watch as one of the light bars runs up her arm slowly. "Ok, I'm going to show you where a few remain that you will have to remove manually. Now that we have managed to free the majority of them on her arm, we will know from now on to apply the cream thicker in places where her body bends naturally. For example, inner elbows and behind the knees, and so forth. The needles were pushed further in these locations because of the movement there."

A small tool emerges out of the same drawer that keeps refilling the bowl I'm using, and then a red light appears. It's light, showing the remaining needles clearly. I take my time, pulling them out one by one. Placing them in a sealed container so that they can't be knocked over if the ship moves abruptly again. After ANDI confirms that the arm is all clear, we move onto the most delicate hands I have ever held.

Instead of pouring the cream over her hand, I simply dunk the whole thing into the bowl, then lift it back out. Holding the bowl under it until it stops dripping, as her hand is drying, I move over to the other shoulder and start the entire process again. I start to peel the hardened cream off her small-boned hands. Suddenly, I stop, horrified.

"ANDI, what the frack…is happening? I'm tearing off her small claws."

"Those are called fingernails, and I was worried that could happen. The needles would have been embedded deeply into the nail base, especially if she was trying to fight them. There is no other way to get them out of there, other than to remove them completely. We will have to bandage the ends of her fingertips until they can regrow. Unfortunately, that is not something that will happen quickly, and they will be very uncomfortable until they grow back. She may not lose them all, but I have a feeling most of them will come off. The nerves in her hands have been damaged worse than the original scan showed. I have been sending our progress to SCOUT and SAGE, but the flares are at their strongest right now and I don't believe they are getting the transmissions. So until we know more, we will proceed onward."

She ends up losing every claw on one hand, but the other two remain. Every piece of hardened cream I peel off her skin removes the needles by the thousands. I can't imagine the anguish she has been in all this time. No wonder she has become unresponsive. I would have found a way to escape too if I had been in her place.

Stopping a moment to stretch, I try to relieve the pressure off my back where I have been leaning over her all rising. ANDI was right about the procedure, making me uncomfortable. The moment I had to put this cream on her breast, I felt myself hesitating. I hated touching her without approval. Up to this point, she has been nothing but a piece of damaged flesh. Now, I'm beginning to see the creature underneath all this damage and she has become strangely beautiful to me.

I have been around the other human females for rotations now and always enjoy their personalities more than their appearances. Their strange dull coloring has never appealed to me, unlike one of my own. I hadn't realized up until now that I compare the majority of females against the unique beauty of my own kind. The vibrant blues and purples of my own people just enhances their loveliness in my eyes. This is the first time I recall even thinking one of the humans was pleasing to the eye.

Shrugging the thought off, I try to concentrate on the procedure before me. I make myself focus on the removal and not the specific part of her body I'm working on. Unfortunately, I have to reapply the cream to her breast twice. As I lift the now needle-free breast up to apply the cream under it. I feel my shaft move as her breast fits fully into my large hand.

Sickened by the thought, I push it away, cursing myself for even looking at her in that way, and I swear the fates are working against me. The needles in her nipples refuse to move and I have to pull them out, one at a time. My face is being forced too close to the temptation of tasting the hardened nipples I'm having to stare down at. Her body and the things I'm having to do to her are going to haunt my dreams forever.

Luckily, her entire face is not damaged as harshly. The needles seem to only be embedded from the bottom of her nose down. Once we remove them, I have to help ANDI burn some out of her nose, ears, and throat. I just hope we are not harming her any worse. The small blisters that immediately appear in her throat have me worried, but ANDI assures me that she is fine.

When I get the majority of her upper body finished, I sit down for a minute, my hands cramping from the tediousness of pulling the stubborn needles out of her skin. This has become a fracking nightmare. I have been stuck a couple of dozen times now from the needles and as sore as they have made my fingers. I can't imagine how she survived the millions. It just shows how strong her will was to live.

"ANDI, once we have all these out, will she have phantom pains or any other side effects from the needles?"

"I have no way of knowing for sure. From what I can gather, the Waldrin normally don't leave survivors and there are zero records out there for me to reference.

"While you have been working on their removal, I have been running a background check on the female. I was happily shocked that I found anything, but disappointed at the same time about what I could find about her past.

"The female's name is Ivy Marie Harper. I'm having a hard time determining the exact date of this information, but she was reported as missing from her mother in the late twentieth century. The report the mother turned in said that her daughter was moving to another state with a boyfriend. The girl's mother received a call from her daughter several hours after they departed, only for it to be interrupted abruptly by some males in the background yelling obscenities.

"Not long after the report was filed, the car they were traveling in and the boyfriend was found alongside the road. The boyfriend had been brutally shot in the head and was pronounced dead at the scene. Not far away, another vehicle and several bodies were found in a nearby field. The only evidence that Ivy was even there was a backpack her mother claimed she would have never left behind. Nothing was missing from the car or the backpack, but there was no trace of Ivy. She was never seen again.

"According to the police records, the mother never stopped looking. The investigators tried to play it off as a runaway case and even put her picture on a milk carton. I will explain what a milk carton is later to you, but the mother was convinced that something terrible happened to her daughter, but that she was still alive. The mother eventually married again some years later to one of the detectives that had been working on the original case. Clear up to the time of her death, the mother never stopped looking for her daughter. I hate reading things like this, it's so sad. The not knowing, I think, would be the hardest to deal with.

"I managed to find a few pictures of Ivy while she was in high school. Here she is, on what they called pajama day. I think it's ironic that she is wearing little blue cartoon characters all over her clothing. They are present in quite a few of the pictures I was able to retrieve from my data bank. As we speak, I'm reconstructing this pattern onto some clothing I'm preparing for her. I'm hoping to administer as much comfort as possible once we get these monstrosities out."

Pulling the holo monitor closer, I gaze at the carefree, smiling girl in what ANDI calls a picture. I flip through a few screens, mesmerized. She radiates life and youth as she stands there with others of her kind. And he is right, it's hard to miss the little blue characters wearing white hats covering her pants. She stares back at me from this picture and I feel my heart hit my chest hard. I vow right there that I will see that smile once again on her face.

CHAPTER 8

A^{vX}

THE LONGER THIS TAKES ME, the madder I'm getting. A few times I have even had to walk out of the room, especially when I start noticing the places where her skin looked practically melted off. Large scars and freshly mended tears mar what I'm sure was once young, perfect skin. I almost quit altogether when ANDI informs me that I am going to have to help him get the needles out of her...private parts. A place no one but her mate should ever see this closely.

"ANDI, I can't violate her like this. We have to find an alternative way to get them out of there."

"AvX, I feel your hesitation, but we are almost finished. You have to think of it as if it was you laying on that table. This is the most sensitive part of her body and those needles are probably causing her more pain there than the majority of the ones on her skin did."

Opening her legs, I step in between them, horrified at what I am doing. The skin on her thighs has also been torn and roughly grafted back together. Her tender folds look chapped and dry as they bleed slightly where the needles have been pressed tightly together. I have peeled every inch of her body, leaving this area last.

Never have I been so happy for someone to be unconscious. She needs to awaken from this nightmare healed, not forced to relive it over and over while she heals. I pour the cream heavily over her folds, separating them with my fingers so that nothing gets missed. I plan on doing this once and never speaking of it again. As far as I'm concerned I pray the female never knows of my assistance in this procedure.

"ANDI, is there a way to keep this from her? What I mean is my part in this removal process. We are going to be around each other often after I drop her off on Darverius, and I would rather it not be uncomfortable for either of us."

"AvX, I will request secrecy to be put in her file, but if asked directly, it's her right to know. I completely understand and would probably feel the same way if I were in your spot. Hopefully, the hows or whys won't be important to her. She will simply be so ecstatic about being painless. None of the other crap will matter."

I feel like the biggest creep as I start lifting the now-dried cream from her sensitive skin. I try to be as gentle and as slow as I can as it lifts away, but her skin still ends up ripping. Tears come to my eyes with each small tear. This part of her body was not made to be abused like this, and I feel like I'm hurting her all over again. I would rather cut my own heart out than harm her any further. ANDI lowers the small device from the ceiling once I have removed all the cream.

"Please tell me this is not going to blister her insides like it did her throat."

"I have set the charge to a minimum. Worst case, we have to do it twice. Don't quit on me yet, AvX. Her body only has a few hundred more of these things left in it now. We are almost done. You have saved this girl's life, AvX, whether you realize it or not."

I smell her flesh burning again, and this time she jerks, even under sedation. Without thinking, I yank the instrument out and insert my fingers into her tender folds, opening her up as wide as I can, trying to feel if the heat has left any damage. I slide my fingers around the inside, determined to make it as impersonal as I can, and failing horribly at it. I withdraw my fingers, happy that I don't feel any needles or blisters left inside of her. Also praying I forget how tight her body was around my exploring fingers.

ANDI finishes the last burn inside the other private hole while I hold her body perfectly still. Once we are done, he runs that red light over her once again slowly. I don't know who is more relieved, me, or ANDI when the light flashes green, and her body is cleared.

I practically collapse into the only chair in the room. Running my hands through my hair, I close my eyes, trying not to relive the crap we have been doing all rising. Glancing back up, I watch her float in the air above the bed. Her long blonde hair hangs limp, dirty, and matted in places. Her skin is red and inflamed. The fresh cuts I inflicted upon her are bleeding freely. Every drop of red that appears tears at my very soul, especially since I know my hands did that to her.

"ANDI, is it too soon to get her cleaned the rest of the way up?"

"No, I was simply allowing you a moment to catch your breath. I was just going to ask you to bring the female into the sanitization room. I have prepared a healing bath for her."

"What about the new cuts and abrasions? Should those be treated first?"

"The bath will help heal those minor injuries. She is not as damaged as your eyes are leading you to believe. Let me put some healing caps on the ends of her fingers where her nails come off and then you can move her."

I take a deep breath and force myself to get up. Reaching through the medical chamber's invisible arms, I lift her away from the bed. Her slight weight settling into my arms has my ruins flashing brightly. I'm confused about their reaction to her.

When her head rolls against my shoulders. I stop to look down, relieved to see that she finally looks relaxed.

Walking into the sanitizer room, I'm shocked to see an enormous tub has risen out of the floor. Lowering her down into the water slowly, I was hoping she would react in some way, but she simply remains lifeless in my arms. The water starts to sizzle and bubble as the jets push the water all around her small frame. I pull her hair up and out of the way before I settle her against the back of the tub.

"ANDI, can you do your magic? I need a way to wash her hair and I don't want to put it in the same chemicals that are in her bath water."

"Give me a moment. I have an idea." A smaller tub emerges from the floor, butting right up against the head of the other one. Water fills it quickly and I lower the long, dirty mass down into it, gently separating the ends, trying to pull the knots out as I work my way upward. Each time I refill the tub, I apply different softening creams into it as I refuse to cut the knots and mats out of her long hair.

If I have learned anything through the rotations from my own mother is the amount of time and currency females are willing to spend on their hair.

My mother would sit for hours at a time braiding and decorating her tresses for special occasions. That thought reminds me of the troubled look Mother had on her face when I left this last time. She said something similar to me as Keida did when I was leaving. *Trust your feelings, even when you think they are not there.* I wonder if they both saw Ivy, or was it a coincidence? Valerian females are known for their visions, but Keida doesn't have any Valerian essence in her genetics that I'm aware of.

The jets shutting down bring me out of my thoughts. I drain both tubs and wring her hair out gently before wrapping it in a long cloth. ANDI provides me with a large soft sheet to wrap around her body and even though it takes me a few tries, I finally get it.

"ANDI, should we put her back in the medical chamber or in one of the other rooms?"

"I think the med chamber would be best for now. Put the rails up on the bed to keep her from falling out. The AllTarra will also awaken soon and Ivy may take comfort in her being in the same area. Also, I have placed some new clothing on the foot of the bed. Hopefully, I have made them easy to remove and put on. These are the first garments I have created in quite some time, and they took longer than I would have anticipated to get correct."

I have the sheet wrapped around her so tight that when I start to lower her down into the bed. I realize I can't get it off. I twist and turn, all the while trying to hold her in one arm. Finally, I manage to pull the sheet off, but what I don't count on is the feeling of her naked skin against my own when I pull her close. My shaft hardens immediately and I gasp as my runes start pulsing all over my skin. My mind reaches out for her instinctively, only to find nothing.

I try my best not to pay attention to the feeling of the soft breast pressed up against my chest. Or the silken texture of her skin underneath my fingertips. She is still like a limp doll in my arms and by the time I get her clothes on her. I feel like I have been in a wrestling match that the other person won.

This has been the longest rising of my life and I'm relieved to finally lay her back on the bed, clean and hopefully pain-free. I gently brush a few long hairs off her face before gathering its long length into my hands. Quickly braiding it loosely, I drape over her shoulder so it doesn't get re-tangled. Hesitantly, I pull my hands away and back off, already missing the feel of her slight frame in my arms. Reluctantly, I pull the blankets up, tucking them around her before turning away.

"AvX, take your rest now. I will notify you once she has awakened."

Exhausted, mentally, and physically, I somehow stumble towards my own quarters. Falling face-first into the immense bed, too tired to even get cleaned up before sleep takes me. I don't know how long I was out before the ship moving abruptly wakes me. "ANDI?"

"Everything is fine, AvX. The asteroid I stationed us on simply bumped up against another one. I have us anchored down firmly and we are not floating off somewhere."

"What if one bumps into us?"

"The Traveler is quick on her feet. I have sensors watching all around us in case one gets close."

"How much longer before we can head home?"

"I don't have that information at this time."

"What about our guest? Has she awakened?"

"No, and it has me slightly concerned. She is fully healed and no longer being held unresponsive by any type of sedation. Technically, she should at least be moving around in the bed, but still nothing."

"Let me get cleaned up and I'll be there momentarily." Every muscle in my body feels sore. Even though I got to sleep deeply for a few hours, I still feel exhausted. Stepping into the Ionizing shower, I stretch my senses out. Hoping to detect something from the female, but everything is still eerily quiet. My stomach growls, but I decide to get some substance after I check on the female. Heading straight to medical as I walk into the room. I'm disappointed that she is laying in the exact same spot I left her in. She hasn't moved a muscle. I run my hand up her arm, peering down at her.

"ANDI, is there a chance we missed something?"

"I scanned her three times while you were resting. I can't find anything that is keeping her in this state. It's like we have her physical body, but her mind is somewhere else."

Hesitantly, I raise one of her eyelids up and wave my hand back and forth in front of it, with zero response. "Let's simply allow her to rest for now. I need food. Then I'll come back in and we'll double-check everything. I agree that her brain's silence is odd and disturbing."

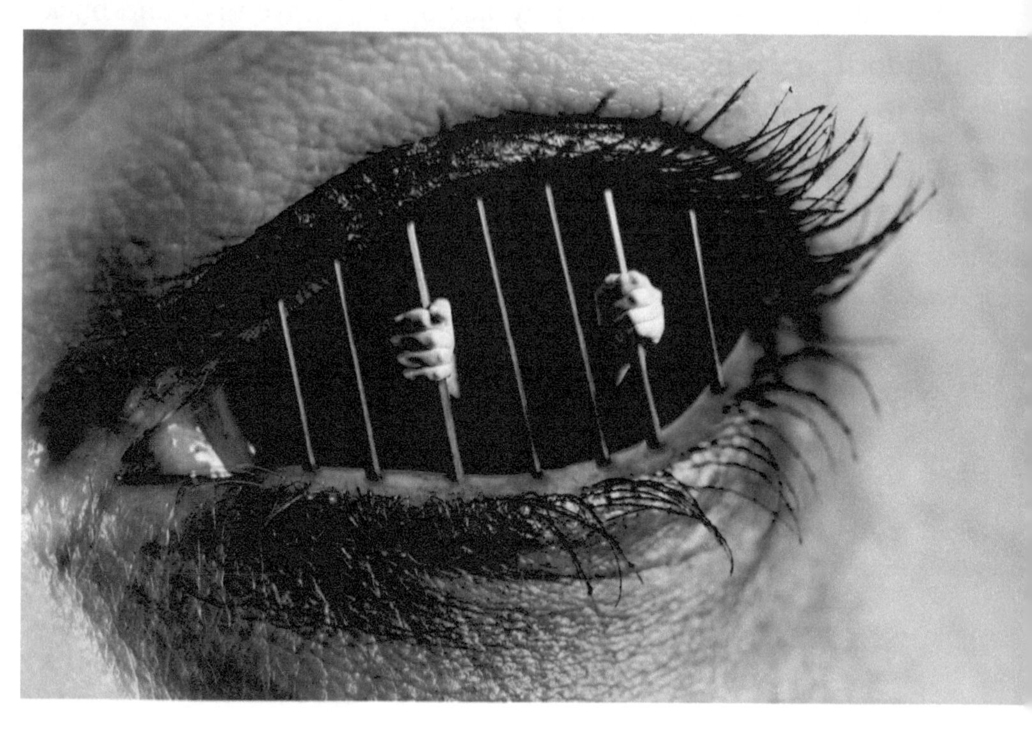

CHAPTER 9

I*vy*

SMOTHERING, I sit straight up, gasping for breath, taking in everything around me in seconds. I'm in some sort of hospital or medical room, but it's wrong. The normal hospital crap like blood pressure monitors or any of that stuff that's usually next to the bed are missing. The room is really quiet and so clean you could eat off the floors. I take a second and glance down at my arms, looking for an IV, not even finding a mark where there could have been one.

I rub my hands all over my skin and the,... pain, it's gone. My skin is still tender, and it looks slightly red, like I have a bad sunburn, but the...pain...I'm not hurting anywhere. My muscles seem a little stiff, but that's it. I curl my legs up under me immediately, noticing the Smurf pajamas I have on are not mine. Wait a minute, I have clothes on.

I raise up a little and look behind the bed, only to stop dead when I see the cage. It was real I didn't make it all up in my head. That cage represents everything I have gone through, all the suffering and the pain. I—those things…they were killing me. Hell, maybe I'm dead now.

Suddenly, my mind starts rewinding. I feel like I'm watching a horror movie from a distance. I see them, the…worms…they were surrounding me. I can hear my own screams echoing throughout that room, the intense agony…then there is nothing.

I float around the room, watching from a distance as they start shriveling up like slugs that had been trapped in the sun. Their screams seemed louder and more intense than mine had. Then something,…or someone,…is there… So many hands, all of them different colors, they pull me away, and that's all I recall before the cage.

I was thrown in and forgotten. Most of the time it was dark and cold…but the pain kept me numb. Time no longer mattered; the minutes and days were all the same. The last place was better, warmer, but I still couldn't move. The pain kept me silent somewhere quiet, a place where I watched from a distance. Then something soft started staying with me, and I didn't feel so alone anymore.

"Mistress, oh, it does my hard drive good to see that you have awakened."

I scream and throw myself off the bed, hunkering down, looking for the voice that seemed to come out of the very walls.

"Be calm, Mistress, you are safe. My name is ANDI and I'm the AI for the ship Traveler you are currently on."

"What the hell ever, computer man! I have already heard the lie *you're safe* once, and I'll be damned if I fall for that one again. Now, if you will just point the way out of here, I will get out of your hair."

The entire wall suddenly disappearing in front of me has me hiding behind the bed. I kneel down when I hear footsteps coming closer. I try to look through the bars of the bed, but I can't see anything.

"Hello?"

I hear a guy's voice and I hunch down further. I ain't doing this shit again. There has to be a way out of here. The wall is still gone, and this may be my only chance to get past him now that he knows I'm awake.

"You don't have to be scared. My name is AvX and I promise no one here will hurt you. Please come out?"

"What the fuck ever," I whisper.

He starts to move towards me and I wait until it sounds like he is just on the other side of the bed before I take off running towards the open wall. I don't make it two steps when the wall solidifies in front of me, blocking my escape.

I grab the first thing I see and turn, ready to fight my way out of here if I have to. Only to stop dead in my tracks when I see him for the first time. In front of me is all the proof I need that my mind has finally snapped. One of my favorite cartoon characters, now full-sized with a rocking hot body and the prettiest blue skin you ever saw, stands before me. The only thing missing is the white hat. Looks like the joke is on me.

I'll play along until he moves closer. "Who are you? How did I get here?"

He starts to move towards me and I throw whatever it was I picked up at him. He ducks it and backs away a few steps.

"Calm down. I understand you're upset."

"Upset, do you even know what that means, Alien Smurf wannabe? Ok, this is how this is going to go. I don't give a shit about you, or the hows or whys. All I want to do is go home and instead of you giving me excuses, you are going to take me or I'm going to make your life a living hell. I'm going to make you so miserable, you are going to wish you would have left me in that fucking cage."

"It's not that easy."

"How am I understanding you?"

"You have a translator chip behind your ear."

"That's great. One more mark against you, bastards. There is this thing called consent, where you ask someone if they want something done to them before you do it. Like, I don't know, would you enjoy being abducted, then thrown into a room for some worm-sucking monstrosities to tear you apart? You know, those sorts of questions.

"Because when you are not asked properly, bad things can happen to you. I will give you an example. You could shrivel up screaming in horrific pain, looking like a big dried-up turd afterward. All I can think of is, apparently, I must not have tasted very good, or maybe I didn't have the right personality. Because after they tired of me, I ended up in that crate being shipped all over god knows where, and…well, that puts us here. Unfortunately for you, my cooperating days have all been used up. You will simply have to hope that your next abductee is more open-minded to having her life stolen away. Now, where were we? Oh yes, the matter of sending me home."

Big, blue and handsome runs his hands through wavy darker blue hair and has the balls to look at me with those bright silver eyes like I'm the problem here.

"Look, I didn't take you from your home and I had nothing to do with what happened afterward. Yes, I bought you,…and yes, I found you in that cage. But I have spent the last rotation trying my best to heal you. A little bit of gratitude would be nice on your end. I have never seen one of your kind act this way."

I throw up my arms. "Act my way! Have you been dropped on your big blue head?" I pick up another object and throw it at him, then another. He just keeps ducking out of the way as he moves back and away from me. "What did you expect me to do? Fall to my knees and grovel at your big ugly feet?" I change my voice and act out. "*Oh, thank you master blue for saving poor little old me…*Yeah, sorry to disappoint, but wrong girl. If you think I'm going to sit here and allow you to hurt me like those others did, you are really mistaken. I understand you feel like I owe you something because you fixed me back up. Now don't think for one minute I'm not grateful for that part, but my trust factor has been trampled on, and I'm all out. I want to go home!"

"Please, let's sit down and we will talk about everything. I can't send you home." He holds his hands up. "Wait a minute before you throw something else at me. We are stuck right now, and can't go anywhere. ANDI will explain it all later, but you have things all wrong. I'm the good guy here."

I actually start laughing after he says that. "Says every serial killer!"

"Fine, whatever, as your kind would say. You're right, I get it. Why trust me when everyone else has hurt you in one way or another? I can feel your emotions are all over the place. You are projecting them so loudly I feel like my mind is about to splinter. You're mad and scared all at the same time and as long as you feel like that, you will never listen to a word I say. I don't know how to prove that you are safe. I'm at a complete loss with the way you are reacting. I wasn't prepared for this at all. The others of your kind had already adjusted to their circumstances, and I met all of them after the fact."

"How many other humans have you kidnapped?"

"Think what you want, but I have gone out of my way to help you medically and spent credits I didn't have to get you out of that fracking crate. At no point did I think this would be your reaction when you awoke. Don't you worry! I will take you to the others as soon as we can leave, but until then, you are just going to have to take my word for it. I can hear your stomach growling from here. You must be hungry. I will return shortly with some substance. Hopefully, this will give you some time to think and calm the frack down."

He stomps past me and right back through the vanishing wall. My legs give out beneath me and I crumble. Tears flow down my cheeks as I realize I'm once again in a situation I have no idea how to get out of. I refuse to fall apart. First thing, I have to get out of this room and find something to defend myself.

I can feel a slight vibration under me, so I know we're in some sort of vehicle. That means it has to have doors or a hatch or something. I just need to find it so I can get out as soon as it stops. I stand up and head towards the disappearing door. It opens for me, shockingly. I stick my head out and look both ways down a narrow hallway.

"Mistress, may I assist you in locating a certain location?"

"You're the talking computer, right?"

"Confirmed, my name is ANDI. All you have to do is say my name and I will reply to your commands."

"Best thing I have heard in a while. ANDI, old buddy, I need to get back home. Can you help me with that?"

"Currently, my database holds the most updated information about your world. I believe if I could show you the things you need to see, this would help make your adjustment easier."

"That's not the answer I was looking for." I walk out into the hallway and look both ways. "Where to start?" I whisper to myself. Turning to the left, I hurry down the long hall. Doors appear along the way, some even open on their own, as I walk by. I stop a few times, glancing inside, only to find most of them empty.

The hall comes to an end and I stand there contemplating how much longer I have until the blue guy finds me again. I jump when the wall disappears completely in front of me, and I feel like I could float away. I walk hesitantly forward, stunned at the sight before me. It looks like I could reach out and touch the stars. There are odd planets in the distance, some with swirling rings like our Saturn, others are just gigantic balls of different colors. I have no idea how long I stand there, but it doesn't take a rocket scientist to realize what I'm seeing isn't in the Milky Way.

A small figure appears out of thin air and hovers in front of me. I step back, startled when he takes his top hat off and bows elegantly. Then he points outward toward space.

"It's quite beautiful, isn't it? It took some maneuvering on my part, but I thought it might be more believable if you could see it yourself."

I reach my hand out, and it passes right through him. "ANDI?"

"At your service. Right now, Ivy, I believe this is the best view in town. I was able to produce a simple force field here temporarily. I won't be able to keep the barrier up much longer, but at least now you know that Master AvX is not lying to you."

"It's,… beautiful, but it's been so terrifying. I don't want to hurt anymore, computer guy. I just want to go home. Mom warned me not to leave, and I didn't listen."

"She loved you very much."

I take my eyes off the view in front of me and look down at him. "How would you know that?"

The wall darkens back down, and I find myself staring at nothing. "Come with me and I will try to explain all that I can. Not to mention, you have a friend who is eager to get reacquainted."

I turn reluctantly; the fight leaving me as I follow behind his floating form. He seems to have the answers to the questions I'm asking, but do I really want to know? I have to smile when I realize why he looks so familiar. He is portraying himself as Dracula. *I have crossed the seas of time to be with you.*

My mom's favorite movie. A tear runs down my cheek as I picture her sitting on the couch with a book in her hand while the radio plays over in the corner. How many nights did we spend in front of that old CD player singing songs and munching on cheese and mustard?

What wouldn't I do to go back in time? Lord, how I regret getting in that car. But I did, and now I'm here on what appears to be a spaceship sitting on a big damn rock, in another solar system, surrounded by things that even monster creators on earth couldn't dream up. I have never been a quitter, but I feel fragile and broken on the inside. The slightest thing and I know I'm going to shatter into a million pieces.

CHAPTER 10

I vy

WE COME RIGHT BACK to the room I had awakened in. I really must have made an impression, or he simply wanted to avoid me because there is a tray laying on the bed, but no Smurf alien.

"ANDI, you notified blue guy that I left the room, didn't ya?"

"There are no secrets on the Traveler, dear. AvX is a gentle soul, all Valerians are naturally. You are lucky it was him you acted so aggressively with and not one of his brothers. Most of them tend to react before thinking. They are all noble males, but can be a handful when together. AvX is the peacemaker."

A familiar coo has me looking around the room. Sitting on a large perch is the most beautiful bird I have ever seen. She is cooing and making clicking noises as she stretches her wings out, prancing back and forth on the ledge beneath her. I gasp when her wings start to shake and her feathers appear to glow brightly.

Walking hesitantly towards her, I'm shocked when she lowers her head for me. "Oh, you are so beautiful…ANDI, was she hurt too?"

"You don't recognize her, do you?"

"No, should I?"

"Yes, she is who was responsible for keeping you alive, especially during the latter part of you being in that cage. She is an AllTarra. As you can see, with that beak and those claws, she is quite the apex predator. They are extremely protective once bonded, and you are one of the few I have any records of them bonding with. They tend to be solitary creatures, even within their own kind. There are rumors and stories of them being able to walk right through walls and even disappearing in front of you. I personally have never witnessed these things, but I'm interested in watching her interact with you. She acts like a pet, but she couldn't be further from that. I wonder if it was because she was raised in captivity, but she didn't bond with the ones who took her. Well, either way, you two were lucky to find each other.

"I don't know at what point she came to be with you in that cage, but she refused to leave you until AvX promised her he would make your pain go away.

"The AllTarra was also injured. A major bone was broken in one of her wings, but she never let that stop her from protecting you. She also was the one who showed AvX, and me, what the primary cause for all your pain was. The only thing I can figure is somehow she was stolen as a chick because they are practically untrappable in the dark forest. AvX was on planet Marin looking for a birthday present for his niece Keida when he came upon a crate vendor. Who had no idea you were in one of the crates until the AllTarra made herself known? That bird saved your life."

"So AvX, my Smurf alien, can talk to her?"

"Not in the sense you are thinking. He projected the feeling of safety and healing toward her and waited until she said that was acceptable. Because if she had not trusted him, she would have killed herself and torn him to pieces before she would have let him take you."

I reach my hand out under her beak and scratch it gently, as she rubs her head against my hand affectionately. I step back when she stretches out her wings and with one flap; she is airborne. Gliding around the room, squawking as I laugh. "Fly, pretty girl. Try those new wings out."

Watching her, I head over to the table where the tray is and lift up the cover. I don't know what type of food it is, but it smells wonderful. I grab what looks like a piece of bread and stuff it in my mouth. It takes me a minute to realize I probably look like a squirrel stuffing my jaws, I'm trying to eat so quickly.

"Ivy don't make yourself sick. There is plenty of food available. You will not go hungry under my watch." I throw a piece of mystery meat up into the air and who I'm now calling Tarra catches it.

"Good girl. Do you want some more? I don't see any field mice on the menu, but this mystery meat isn't too awful." She swoops down so fast I feel my hair move away from my face right before she settles next to me.

I hesitantly hand her a small piece, hoping she doesn't take a nip out of my fingers by mistake, but she is extremely gentle. I feed her a few more pieces before she moves over and starts grooming herself. When I start to get up, she reaches over with one wing, pulling me back down, then hops up onto my lap. I grunt as she bounces on me because she is much heavier than she appears. Her sharp claws poke me through these thin pants, but because she seems to be looking for something, I don't move her.

"What is it, Tarra? Whatcha see, pretty girl?"

She tilts her head one way, then another, before settling down and tucking her head into her wing.

"ANDI is she ok?"

"This is her way of showing you affection and trust. The fact that she is willing to let you hold her while she sleeps, when she is the most vulnerable, is amazing. Did you know that she would stretch her wings out over you to keep you warm at night? This AllTarra has been mistreated and abused. That would have made most animals mean and mistrusting, but she must have seen something in you worth saving."

"Since I'm not going anywhere, you said you were going to show me something about home."

"Ivy, you have been through so much already. I'm not sure this is the right time."

"ANDI, I'm tired of being in the dark. Please, don't lie to me or sugarcoat things. I can't prepare for tomorrow if I have no idea what's going on around me."

A large screen appears out of the wall, floating right in front of my face. I almost cry out when I see my mom appear on it. She is standing behind a podium, talking to a crowd of people. I can't hear what she is saying, but the captions at the bottom of the screen show what she is talking about...*me*. Before she walks off, there is a picture of me right before I left, standing next to her. In my holey blue jeans and a crop top, with bandanas all over my legs. I look like a rag doll.

She is on TV asking if anyone has seen her daughter. Tears flow down my face as newspaper clippings flash with my face on them. Each time something new comes on ANDI shows me the dates and times. I watch my mother slowly get older on the screen. I laugh and then cry uncontrollably when I see the announcement of her marriage, then her death certificate.

The world continues on, but then it is like watching the movie *The Day after Tomorrow*. My world is destroying itself frame by frame and then it's just gone. Tarra wakes with my tears and rubs her head against my chin, trying to comfort me. I pull her close and cry into her soft feathers as she coos softly. This whole time ANDI never says a word. He simply shows me clips of my world, …Earth and the outcome.

"ANDI, how long was I…I don't really know what to ask."

"I have no way of knowing exactly how long you were in stasis, or even exactly who took you. Thankfully, your youth helped to keep you healthy and as preserved as possible. Commander DaR, AvX's father, thought that they destroyed all the slave ships, but apparently, some were either already in the outer quadrants and were undetectable, or they had previously sold their cargo off.

"I was on Earth for thousands of years myself and I saw it rise and then fall personally. If I had a heart, it would have broken the day of its ultimate destruction. I know you think that you have nowhere to go, but that is inaccurate, as there are several of your kind alive and prospering on Darverius. The good part is your youth will help you adapt better than if you had been older. I'm sorry for your loss and the pain that you are experiencing. I would love to promise you that it will all be smooth sailing from this point on, but even with my knowledge, I cannot foresee the future. You should try to get some rest. The AllTarra is still healing, and your heart is heavy."

He clicks off the screen, and the room darkens down. I pull Tarra close as the tears flow freely. I sob so hard it's taking my breath, all that I have missed out on…simply because of my bad decisions. I'm truly alone now. Never again will I get to call Mom or hug Tommy when I've had a bad day. How do you accept this? Even witnessing it all with my own eyes, seeing the planets outside. What happens to me now?

CHAPTER 11

I^{vy}

I CRIED until my stomach was hurting and had just closed my eyes that the entire ship shakes like it has a chill or something.

I hear heavy footsteps heading my way and I grab Tarra, pulling her in close. She lets out an aggravated huff because I interrupted her beauty sleep.

Climbing out of the bed slowly, I back away into a darkened corner. The big blue guy barrels through the disappearing wall. Tarra flares her wings out aggressively. Her feathers brightening the room with a flash of light.

"Control that bird, Ivy. It's just me! ANDI, I have been screaming your name all the way down the hall. We are taking fire. How did your sensors not pick that ship up before they got right on top of us?"

"I apologize, AvX. My only excuse is that our cloaking device either failed or we have a tracker somewhere on the ship. I was caught up in the past and was assured that my sensors would see anything approaching."

"It's too late for excuses now. Secure the girl. I'll head to the control room and see if I can keep them off of us long enough for you to launch us off this rock."

"Where do you want me to put her, AvX? I am no longer equipped with those types of restraints. When I was remodeled, they were removed. For that matter, we have few weapons to defend ourselves with. The Traveler is a cargo ship, not a battle-cruiser."

"Frack, I don't know, ANDI… Frack it,… Ivy get in the cage. I know it's not where you want to be, but right now it's the only place you won't get thrown around if this goes bad. Take the bedding and the pillows with you and stuff them around you the best you can."

"The hell I am! What are you trying to do, make it easy for the next guy to pack me off, because I'll already be packaged and ready to go? I'm not getting in there ever." If looks could kill, I would have become melted goo on the spot.

"You will if you don't want to die, tuck her into your arm and crawl in. This isn't a discussion. I won't lock the door, but it's all I have to offer you right now safety-wise."

The ship tilts hard to its side, and I can tell if I don't go in on my own, he is going to shove me in. I tighten the hold I have on Tarra and crawl back into this— *I'm not going to think about it… this is just a place to be more secure.* "Don't you dare lock that door!"

He shakes his head and clips the door shut before turning on his heel and running away. Tarra is practically wrapped around me as I sit on the floor, rocking us back and forth. She coos as she bumps her head against my chin. I take a second to look down at her huge trusting eyes and I don't know how, but I start to relax. Her features are a mix of owl and hawk, and she is beyond beautiful.

"Such a pretty girl, ain't ya?"

I start humming a song that my mom sang to me when I was little. I don't know if I'm doing it for her or me at this point. The floor suddenly starts shaking so hard my teeth are rattling. I scream out when we tilt hard the other way, this time we are thrown against the side of the cage. The door pops open and I put Tarra down and crawl out. She starts to follow me, but I pull the door closed before she can. "Stay here, pretty girl. I'll be right back."

I run over to where her perch was and pull it out of the clear container. It swings back and forth on hinges and I know if I can get this in the cage, she will be much safer on it than she was in my arms.

I open the cage back up and crawl in with the perch in my hand, anchoring it between two slots in the side. I gently pick her up and put her on it. "Tarra, stay here. I don't want you hurt. If you are out there flying around, something might fall and hit you." I kiss her beak and back out. Expecting her to come after me, but I swear it is like she understands I am trying to keep her safe.

I grab onto things as I make my way out of the room. I have no idea where AvX might be, but I can't just sit in that cage and hope for the best. The door opens and I look out into the hall. I know if I go left it's a dead end, so I head to the right. I can hear him cussing before I even find the room he is in.

"Shut your emotions down, Ivy, and get in here and help me if you're going to roam all over the place. ANDI, ANDI!" He hits the wall. "FRACK, he is not responding. He must have been knocked offline. Or who the frack knows at this point? Either way, we are screwed because the Traveler was not supposed to be flown without an AI to assist, and I have very little flight experience myself."

"What do you want me to do?"

"You have any other skills besides being an ungrateful degenerate?"

"Nope, at this moment I believe that's the only thing I can put on my resume as a true skill. Now we can stand here and argue while they shoot us down, or you can tell me what to do to help before we crash. I've had a couple of really bad days here lately and I would rather not add to them."

"Since you're not going anywhere, sit down and strap in. RaZ flew the Traveler by himself when the original AI went rogue. So I know there is a way to do this. I just can't find the controls." He hits a button and shouts. "RaZ, SCOUT, Falcor, someone, come in. Frack, I have sent multiple messages out, but the solar flares are still blocking everything. We don't have a chance if I don't get us off this rock. The asteroid shifted its position when they fired at us the first time and that's the only thing saving our asses right now."

The Blue Smurf dude starts throwing things all over the place and pulling pieces off a huge panel that has tons of buttons on it.

"Hey, you ripping and tearing isn't going to fix this. I'm sure there is a user's manual somewhere."

"A what?"

"A book, you know, full of pieces of paper that show us some of the things included in this model."

"No, pieces of paper, but… See if that holo pad beside you will come on."

"Am I supposed to know what that is?"

He reaches over me and touches a small pad that has miraculously not fallen on the floor yet. I can help but yelp when the entire ship tilts hard to the side and I can hear it scraping against something. "Oh, god, oh god."

"Quit praying and find a way to help me."

"Are you bossy much? Shit, you know just how to piss a girl off. Ok, this pad thing is all lit up, now what? I can't read freaky, deaky Dutch scribbles."

He looks up at the ceiling. "ANDI, if you are floating around out there, we could sure use your assistance."

He no more says that than the scribbles on the pad turn into English and a schematic pops up. "Ok, I don't know what magically happened, but give me a second." I scroll around the page looking for a lever or anything that talks about flight controls. "Here, look at this!"

Taking the pad out of my hand. "You're a genius." He grabs me, kissing me quickly before he reaches under the dash to pull a lever. Our seats move back as a set of controls comes out of the floor and everything on the panel lights up.

"Yes, we got this." He hits a few buttons and I feel the ship start to shake. I grasp onto my chair as he pulls a lever back and we shoot forward. My whole body is tingling. I'm not sure if it's from the rush of almost dying or that… kiss.

CHAPTER 12

Ivy

I SEE a few bright flashes across the windshield, viewer, or whatever the thing is in front of me. "What are those?"

"Solar flares. Right now, they are a blessing and a curse. The bounty hunters have lost our trail because the flares are messing with the signals, but they are also blocking ours."

I start to get up and ease away from him. "What have you done to have bounty hunters after you?"

He glances up at me and by the look on his face, that was not the right question. "Oh, let me see, I picked up a random ungrateful human from a vendor and it's been chaos ever since. Sit down before you get hurt again. With ANDI offline, I don't have the extra hands to heal you if you do."

"Why did you help me? Since the moment I opened my eyes, you have made it plain that I am a burden. If that was the case, why did you take me at all?"

He hits a couple of buttons and then turns towards me. "I wasn't prepared for you."

I start to say something, and he holds his hand up, stopping me.

"I was under the impression your kind were all the same in temperament and I was not prepared for your anger or your distrust upon your awakening. You are not a burden, and I apologize that I have made you feel that way. The moment I saw you in that cage, the rage that overcame me at how you had been treated was all-consuming. I would have torn that planet apart to save you and not just because it was my duty to do so. Your body was,...well, I didn't know if you would make it, and in my mind. I pictured you awakening slightly differently than you did. I'm glad that you don't remember the horrors after you were attacked and lost consciousness. And I would love for us to start over."

He sticks his hand out for me to shake, and I look at him hesitantly, refusing to touch him. Have I misunderstood this whole situation?

"My name is AvX. I'm the eighth son of Commander DaR, the protector of Darverius, also grandson of scholar and elite

Tyberius. My mother's name is Aaya. She is the second in line of succession on my home planet, AvXuqem."

"Wow, you're all that and some, huh? I'm just plain old Ivy Harper, daughter of Becky, and just your normal southern trailer trash Earth girl. I mean, let's talk about this for a second. What did you think was going to happen after all I had been through? That I was going to open my eyes in a strange room with an alien standing over me and yell out, *my hero*? Are you delusional or naïve? How would you react if you were in my place?"

He pulls his hand back and I can see that once again he is not happy with me, but I have made him look at this differently. "Look, all we're doing is rubbing each other the wrong way. I'm sorry that I haven't lived up to your make-believe image of the human female, and to be honest I will probably just keep disappointing you. I seem to have that effect on the people who have been good to me. I would love to say, just drop me off at the next bus station and I'll get out of your hair, but that's no longer an option."

I don't know why all of a sudden I feel like crying. Why do I do this? Why do I strike out at the people, aliens, who are only trying to save or take care of me? He is just sitting there looking at me like I'm a puzzle he is trying to solve.

"Ivy, you have every right to feel confused and lost. As you said, we have not started off on our best foot. I don't know what to say or do at this point. All I can do is give you my word that I won't dump you somewhere to fend for yourself. I will find a way to get you back to the others of your kind. With that being said, I appreciate your help and quick thinking when it comes to the controls, but there is no reason for you to remain up here with me. You should return to the med bay and rest. Your body has been through a lot of trauma. You don't need to add to it by arguing with me."

Tears pool up in my eyes, but I refuse to let him see them. I stand up quickly without saying anything else and walk back down the hall. I hear Tarra squawking as I get closer. The door opens and I walk over to the cage, popping the door open so she can come out.

Instead of flying out like I thought she would, she settles down instead. "Come on, pretty girl, you wanna get out of there for a while?" She stretches her wings out only to re-wrap them tightly around her own body before she tucks her head going back to sleep. I stand up and grab another blanket off the bed, wrapping it around me, before crawling back into the cage with her. I lay down on the floor in front of her perch, replaying the conversation I just had with AvX. Wrapped up like a taco, I let the tears flow as I continue to feel sorry for myself.

Suddenly, something stabbing me in the arm has me jerking up. I pull the blanket away and even though it takes me a few seconds, I finally find it. It's so small it looks like a sharp hair. I draw it out slowly. The lights flicker in the room and when they flash back on. I see several of these slivers laying throughout the cage's floor.

I scoot back out and shake the blanket. A few of those things float to the floor. Being barefoot, I cautiously walk around them as I look for a way to sweep them up before someone else steps on them.

I open every drawer and cabinet in the room, only to find nothing. There are several buttons on one wall, and hesitantly, I hit one of them. Then shriek when the wall lights up. Something immediately starts playing on the screen, but there is no noise. It takes me a minute to realize that AvX is standing over someone, or thing, pulling stuff out of their skin with tweezers. *Ugh, yuck.* I look around, realizing it's showing this room.

AvX looks tired, and several times he even stops to stretch. He moves slightly to the right, and that's when I see it...*me.* He is working on me! My skin is horribly red, and there are small streams of blood all over what's left of me. If it wasn't for seeing my own face, I would never have dreamed that the thing laying on that bed was me.

I'm a fucking mess. What did they do to me after I passed out from the pain? No wonder he thought I would be more appreciative. He really did save my life. I'm such an ungrateful bitch. I'm not good at apologizing, but it looks like I'm gonna have to suck it up and put my big girl pants on. I suck at swallowing my pride, but I owe him at least that much.

I watch him for a few more minutes before I hit the button to turn the screen off. From what I can tell, I was covered in those little needles. I refuse to let my mind dwell on how they got there.

That was yesterday and this is now. Tears run down my face as I give myself this little mental pep talk.

I'm never going home. I'm never going to see my mom ever again. I have been tortured, and I have been healed. There are only two ways to view this new world I have been thrown into. Either I can go towards the light and see what it has to offer or I can be the mirror only looking back at what I can't change.

I vy

SUDDENLY NERVOUS, I pull my hair around and start to undo the braid, combing my fingers through it as I work through the knots. I stop when I realize that AvX must have been the one to also fix my hair and dress me. I'm such a shit. He could have easily left me in that cage. I'm no one to him. Instead, he went out of his way to heal and provide for a complete stranger. Who has done nothing but bitch and complain since I opened my eyes.

Looking down at the soft pants I have on, my heart jerks when it hits me. He was trying to give me comfort in any way he could. ANDI must have found some old pictures with me wearing my

Smurf pajamas, and between the two of them, somehow they made these. Damn, thank you isn't going to be good enough.

I stand here looking around, knowing that if the tables had been turned. I would not have done the same for him. How unselfish do you have to be to take on... *me?* Before I chicken out, I make myself walk out of the room and back toward AvX.

He doesn't move when I approach, just keeps staring down at what looks like a map, and I know he heard me coming. "AvX?"

He turns slowly. "What?"

"I'm...sorry. There is no excuse for my behavior. I know I have not acted, or behaved, as I should, but... I want, no, I need to thank you for saving my life."

He bites his lips together and I swear it looks like he is trying to stop from laughing. He looks down for a second, but when he lifts his head back up, the smile that graces my presence nearly takes my breath. That is, until he opens his mouth. "That was hard for you, wasn't it?"

"I won't apologize for simply reacting, but yes, I have never been good at eating my own words. If you would allow it, I would love for us to start over. Maybe on a more common ground than you being an alien, and me being a backwoods human. You took the time to save a complete stranger, and you are still providing me with food and a roof over my head. Besides pushing a few of my buttons, you have been the perfect host, and I have acted like an ungrateful, spoiled brat. I won't say that it won't happen again, as

I tend to strike out when cornered, confused, or hurt, but I promise to try."

His smile gets bigger and there is no missing that adorable ass dimple on his cheek. "I can feel your sincerity, Ivy, and I appreciate it. I have not been at my best either. The last few risings have been quite trying for both of us. If you would like to take a seat, maybe we can attempt this new truce you have drawn up for us."

I hesitantly sit down. Suddenly the room feels tense and now that I have apologized. I don't know what to say. "Did you figure out where ANDI went?" I blurt out.

"Yes, and no. I think he is still running things in the background. But the solar flares are messing with his main hard drives. This is actually all my fault. All ships are grounded when the flares are at their most intense. Overconfident in our flight pattern, I believed we were flying away from them and they would no longer be an issue once we got out of range. So this all could have been prevented if I had waited a few more risings, but then I wouldn't have found you. Once again, the fates and the Lord of Light put me exactly where I was supposed to be."

I stop to assess what he said. *Am I exactly where I'm supposed to be? Damn, that's a hard pill to swallow.*

"What are you thinking right now? Your emotions are all over the place."

"You have said that a few times to me, your feelings… What does that mean, can you feel me somehow?"

"Ahhh, it's my turn to say I'm sorry. I take for granted a lot of times that others just know things. I'm a Valerian. My people, or I should say my mother's people, as I'm half Darverian, we are more sensitive to emotions than other species. Many of our females see visions, or dreams…most of the time it's triggered by touch, so if they are overly sensitive, they shy away from strangers. The males can feel extreme emotions. I have learned to push others out, but there are times you project yours rather forcefully and I can't not feel them."

"So, not only have you had to deal with my mouth, but all the craziness going through my head, too." I could crawl under something and hide right now. "If I was going to pick a super-power, AvX. That wouldn't have been it. I don't *people* well, now I'm gonna have to add that I don't *alien* well either." I hold my hands up using air quotations for those two words.

"You will adjust. The others have, but no two ever handle things the same."

"Is that where we are headed right now, back to this Darverius?"

"I wish that were the case, and there is no reason for me to hide this from you any longer, but we are lost."

"Lost, as you don't know where to go, or where we are headed?"

"Lost as in lost! The navigation system is completely offline and I can't read these maps. I have always been a passenger, and never even had the urge to learn how to operate one of these ships like all my other brothers."

"What do we do?"

"Oh, these flares will settle down eventually, and then hopefully we are in range to get a message out, or ANDI decides to kick back on."

"You are way too calm about this. I mean, we could float out here forever."

"If I was anyone else's son, that thought may have crossed my mind, but not with my father. My father would turn this universe inside out to find one of his sons. I understand it all sounds bad right now, but we are lucky enough to have all the comforts of home right here on the ship. We just have to sit back, relax, and wait."

"What about the bounty hunters? You know the whole reason we are lost in the first place? How did they find us? If they did it once, don't you think they can do it again?"

He throws the maps down he was looking at and runs his fingers through his dark blue hair. "One problem at a time, Ivy. My nerves are shot and honestly, I have no idea how they tracked us, or what to do about it. I know the tracker isn't in you or the AllTarra because of all the scans we used in medical."

"What about the cage? I'm assuming you brought me here in it?"

"The cage, frack. Why didn't I think of that?" We both jump up at the same time and I bump hard into him. He grabs me, pulling me close before I fall. The moment my hands touch his skin, these beautiful silver marks light up all over him. I trace one on his bare arm. When I glance up, his eyes are closed. He must have felt something because he lets go of me suddenly. Then motions for me to go ahead. The moment my hands leave his flesh, the lights go away.

Just as I start to ask what those were, the ship tilts hard again, and I'm knocked to my knees. AvX grabs me, pulling me up before shoving me back into the chair I just got out of.

He rushes to the panel, hitting a few buttons, and I feel the ship straighten back up. Then all of a sudden it feels like we are being pulled backward. "AvX, what's happening?"

"They have locked onto the ship and are pulling us in. You need to hide."

"Who?"

"If I was a betting male, I would say it's the bounty hunters."

"What about you?"

"They don't want me... Ivy, look at me. I know you're terrified, but you don't have time to panic. Two doors down are the captain's quarters. There is a closet to your left as soon as you enter the room. Go there and lock the door. No one can open that panel but me."

I get up and run down the hall. Just as I start to open the second door, I hear Tarra squawking. She is trapped in that cage. I sprint towards the medical chamber waving my hand hoping the wall disappears as I'm headed that way. Luckily, it does. I slide on my knees over to the cage, pulling the door open. Tarra flies out and I turn to head back to the room where he told me to hide.

The moment the wall opens, my ears start to pop, and I hear multiple footsteps coming my way. Then AvX's voice. "I already told you; I don't have a female on this ship. I bought an AllTarra on Marin and they let me keep the cage."

"Shit! Shit!" I scramble around, trying to find a place to hide. All the cabinets are too small for me to squeeze into, and the rest of the room is completely open. I dart behind the bed and crouch down, hoping they can't see my feet. Tarra squawks and screeches as she flies around the room.

The wall opens. "See, there is nothing here but the AllTarra." One of them must have started into the room. "I wouldn't go in there if I were you. The AllTarra are extremely territorial. She will tear you apart."

Another voice echoes through the room. "Search the ship. I don't want a cushion unturned. The female has to be here."

"This is uncalled for; do you know who I am?"

"Actually, we do, Valerian. That's why I know that female is somewhere. Your kind are too predictable. There is no possible way you would have left a female behind. The fact that you have the cage in the ship's medical chamber only proves my point. If it had just been the bird, you would have taken it out of the cage in the cargo hold. If you don't give the female up willingly, you will also be taken."

"Take this ship, and my father will destroy you."

"I don't care who your father is, Valerian. This is my territory."

"You have been given your options, the fact that you are protesting so adamantly once again proves you have something to hide."

I had gotten so wrapped up in what they were saying to each other that I missed one of them walking further into the room. Tarra stretches her wings out and flashes what feels like a shock wave throughout the room. It hits me, knocking me down and away from the place I was hiding. In an effort to keep me safe, she just revealed the fact that I am here.

"There she is. Grab her," I hear a voice yell out. Multiple hands grab me and I scream out, struggling and kicking. I see AvX fighting against what looks like a werewolf, a large gash already across his chest. I shout out his name when I see one of them sneaking up behind him and just as he turns. The one he was fighting takes advantage of the distraction and hits him over the head hard. He crumbles to the ground.

I struggle that much harder, trying to free myself as I call out AvX's name. I hear one of them yell 'someone shoot that bird' and just as a shot goes off, the wall solidifies, separating her from us. I can still hear her screeching, so she is still alive.

The werewolf guy walks up, grabbing my face in his hand. "Calm yourself, female, you will not be harmed, but be warned we will retaliate if you strike one of us."

"You bastard, you killed him!" I cry out as the tears flow down my cheeks, still struggling to get away from the one holding me.

The one in charge looks down at AvX and then back at me. He drags a long nail down my neck and in between my breasts. "What are you willing to do to keep me from killing him?"

"Leave him alone, dog breath. You wanted me, well, here I am. It's not going to matter what I say or offer, you are going to do whatever you want either way."

He growls and I pull back and away from the slobbering canines in front of me. "Your mouth can be put to better use than the foul words coming out of it. I'm feeling rather giving at the moment, don't give me a reason to become angry. The Waldrin have issued a bounty I simply can't resist for you alive or dead." He kicks AvX's foot. "I wonder what he is worth to his kind. Take them both and lock the ship up."

"Wait, you don't want him. It's me you want."

"True. If he proves unwanted or unworthy, then we will simply dispose of him at a later time. But this cargo ship is quite valuable, so I'm betting he is worth something. We will tow the freighter with us either way."

One of the dogs picks AvX up effortlessly and throws him over his shoulder. I don't say anything else as they shove me down the hall towards what looks like a hole in the side of the ship. I push back again when the one who has been holding me this whole time grabs both of my arms and manhandles me across what feels like a rubber tube.

I don't have much time to see anything before I'm thrown into a darkened room. I start to stand up, only to be knocked back down by AvX's body as he is thrown at me. We slide forcefully against a wall, my whole body now aching and bruised by the impact. The door closes, and it takes me a second for my eyes to adjust to what light is in the room.

Pulling myself out from under AvX, I walk around only to find absolutely nothing besides a hole in the floor and it doesn't take a rocket scientist to figure out what that's for.

AvX groans and I run back to his side. I lift his head up gently and place it on my lap. "Hey, take it easy. You have a huge bump on your head and these cuts are bleeding pretty bad." I run my hands over him, looking for any other injuries, but these two seem to be it. I rip the bottom off one of my pant legs and put pressure against the cuts on his stomach. The material quickly turns dark blue, but his skin lights up again, just not as brightly as before. I can't stop the tears from flowing down my cheeks. I'm scared to even think what the hell could happen next, because the way things are going, it won't be good.

I look down at his bruised face, one eye already swelling shut. He would have never been hurt like this or even put in this position had he left me in that cage. I wish that AvX had never found me. Look at what's happened to him just because he was trying to do the right thing. My tears hit his chest and I swear I hear him hiss. I can't see him well, but it looks like his cuts are healing before my eyes. This just makes me cry harder because I know my mind is simply searching for a light at the end of this tunnel.

"You can't die on me, AvX, not many girls get rescued by their favorite cartoon character." I pull him up against me as high as I can and rock him back and forth. The weight of his body comforting against mine. I lay my head on his shoulder as I wrap my arms around his body, keeping pressure on his wounds.

I jump at every noise, the constant growls and things slamming have me on pens and needles. After what feels like hours, AvX's heart isn't beating as rapidly, and he seems to be resting easier. I'm worried that he hasn't awakened yet, but it's not like I can do anything else for him.

A light suddenly comes on and I blink rapidly as my eyes adjust. The door opens and one of them comes in. I got an up-close view of their faces before, but this is the first time I have had time to look at the total package. Yep, full-blown werewolf, big ass teeth and claws to match, not including that he smells like a wet dog.

He throws a blanket at me and then puts a tray down on a table I hadn't noticed coming out of the wall. I don't move, I just hug AvX closer. "He needs a doctor."

"The Valerian will either wake up or he won't. You need to be worried about yourself. Once those Waldrin get ahold of your fragile body, you will be praying for a quick death."

I don't say another word, as he stands tall above me until he kicks AvX's foot again. He snarls when he sees me pull him closer. "Leave him alone, dog. You act all big and bad now, but you had him outnumbered four to one. He was kicking your hairy ass until your buddies jumped in."

He snarls, drool stringing from his lips. "For a moment, I contemplated keeping you for myself. You are young and relatively healthy, possibly even a good breeder. But it would take me too long to train you and I like my women willing."

I start laughing hysterically. "Gonna train me… you're the fucking dog and you're gonna train me." I can't stop laughing. I swear it's like my mind has snapped and somewhere my realities have swapped. Talking hot-bodied Smurfs, big ass dominating dogs. Pet owls, worms with legs. What the hell is next? I laugh so hard I'm practically screaming. The dog shakes his head and walks out of the room.

CHAPTER 14

S AGE

"SCOUT, have you been able to contact ANDI after that last super flair?"

"Negative, SAGE. Multiple messages have been sent, with no response. I believe it's pastime to notify the Commander."

"I should have told him the moment Master AvX bought the female, but I foolishly thought they were on their way home. My feelings are beginning to override my processors. SCOUT, when you got the intel about the human female, did it mention who the bounty hunters were that took the job?"

"No, it was still in the bidding process. There could be multiple possibilities in that sector, as pirating seems to have free rein there. Foolishly, Master AvX traveled out of our Commander's jurisdiction. DaR could be reprimanded for interfering if he goes after him personally. Let me invite Falcor into this conversation."

"Present, already."

"Falcor, I have sent you all the information we have available to us. Can you advise us further?"

He is quiet for a moment. "ANDI is operational, but in his base form. His hard drive took a hit from that last super flare. He reacted quickly enough to back up his mainframe, but until the flares calm, his processor won't allow him to fully re-engage. What intel I could gather, The Traveler had its manual controls deployed. Hold momentary…This is interesting. Apparently, it is being towed as we speak. In half a rising, it will be completely out of my radar's range."

"Falcor, the Traveler is a large cargo transport. Can we narrow down who in that area would have a ship capable of towing it? Can't ANDI do anything? What about AvX and the girl?"

"I'm not picking up any life forms on board, and the ship that has attached to him…is blocking me completely. Their distance and the solar flares are hindering my sensors. They picked a dangerous time to travel."

"How far out are they?"

"At their current speed, I will lose them altogether by this darkness."

"Is EvO anywhere near?"

"I lost direct contact with the Destroyer during that last super flare, but at that time, he was completely on the other side of our solar system. Also, the Explorer is currently in the repair dock, so it can't be deployed. ViN has the only other long-range personal shuttle that could make the journey and it's currently on Targres Four. He isn't answering Tordan's hails, either. Either he is out of range, or the flares are messing with his personal comm."

"Gentlemen, there has to be something we can do. If I report this to DaR, without some sort of plan, he is going to flip out. Do you know how often he threatens to unplug me? I'm already dreading this conversation."

SCOUT speaks up. "SAGE, I would never allow you to be erased."

If I would have been installed with a heart, mine would have skipped a beat with all the emotions I felt with his words. I set the recording so I can listen to him say that again later and make myself concentrate on the conversation he is having with Falcor.

"Falcor, I have been running scans on the solar flares and I believe there will be a break in them momentarily. This could provide a smaller shuttle ample time to get out of harm's way and if they can dock with ANDI without the other ship's knowledge, this may provide the assistance AvX requires. Tordan should be able to reboot ANDI easily once on board."

"Acknowledged, I will send the repair bots out to refit one of the newer shuttles for the extended trip immediately. Additionally, I sent out a notification for Commander DaR and Tordan to report to my main deck. I'm awaiting confirmation of their arrival."

DaR

"I'M GOING to have every one of you unplugged. All three of you have overstepped your programming and direct orders. My son is missing, and you have waited until now to notify me. This is absolutely unacceptable and there will be repercussions. The very second these flares are over; I expect a detailed head count on each one of them. Do I make myself clear?"

SCOUT stands protectively behind SAGE as she wrings her hands nervously, her small holo form flickering in and out. He picks her holo form up pulling her back against his solid frame, his eyes flash red before he speaks. "Commander DaR, we informed you the moment we had accurate information about the situation. Between the three of us, I believe we have found a solution."

I wave my hand for him to continue.

"A personal shuttle is being outfitted to make the long-range flight as we speak. If my calculations are correct, two of you could successfully get to ANDI within half a rotation. Unfortunately, there will be no extra room for large-scale weapons and we have no idea how many occupy the ship that is now towing them further away. I have to dissuade you, Commander DaR, from personally going into that region because you don't have jurisdiction and this could become a problem at a later date if Commander ZoD is not given a courtesy call."

"Duly noted, SCOUT, but I will be on that shuttle. If you can contact him, inform him of the circumstances. If not, we will blame it on the flares. Tordan?"

"Let me notify Luna that I'm leaving and I will meet you at the shuttle bay. Let's say ten minutes."

"SAGE!"

"I have already notified Mistress Kira. She is on the line as we speak."

The large holo comes on. Kira is turned away from the main comm unit in the house, talking to Ickis. "If you eat the tops of those flowers again, young man, I'm going to turn you into a belt. I have waited forever to see those bloom. Pick something else to gnaw on."

"My love."

Kira turns around at the sound of my voice. "Oh, DaR honey, SAGE just told me what was going on with AvX. You go do your thing, and come back to me in one piece."

"I hate leaving you overnight, but I don't have a choice. I feel like I need to take care of this personally."

"Of course you do. I would expect nothing less. Now, don't worry about me, I'll head down to Brit's around dinnertime. I have a few things I need to finish here in the garden before I leave. Ickis is here even though he has been in trouble all morning, and SAGE has already locked the place down. I will be fine."

"I'm not comfortable with you traveling there alone. I will have XuL come and retrieve you. I would prefer you to stay with them until I return."

"If it makes you feel better, that's fine. Now stop worrying about me and go get that sweet boy of yours."

"I love you, my little human."

"Love you too, my alien."

CHAPTER 15

A vX

I sit straight up. "Ivy!"

"I'm here. Lay back down before you start bleeding again."

"You were supposed to hide!"

"Never been good at doing what I'm told. Thought you figured that out already."

Small arms pull me back down, and I relax as her thoughts brush against mine. She is scared and relieved I have awakened. I look around, barely able to see anything in the dim light.

"How are you feeling?"

I reach up, rubbing the knot on my head, wincing at the instant pain. Pressure against my stomach has me looking down at one of Ivy's small hands. "Frack, like I got my ass handed to me. Are you ok?" I turn, trying to see her in the darkness.

"Quit moving around and lay back. I'm bruised up, but other than that, ok. You, on the other hand, took one hell of a beating, but they knew you were there. The big guy didn't come out of it completely unscathed. However, you never had a chance. They outnumbered you badly."

I settle firmly back against her, not missing the feeling of her soft breasts pushed up against my back. "Here, help me up. I'm too heavy for you to hold me like a youngling."

She pulls against me. "Your weight isn't bothering me at all, so sit still. The wounds on your stomach have just stopped bleeding and I would rather them not reopen because you're being stubborn."

I stop moving and try to rest for a minute. "What have I missed while I was out? I'm shocked they put us in here together."

"Not much, dog breath came in threatening me, you know, with the usual abductee speech."

I have to hold my stomach when what she says strikes me funny. "I didn't know there was a standard speech."

"Amateur, I can tell this is your first time."

"Did they capture the AllTarra?"

"No, Tarra is still with ANDI as far as I know."

"Tarra?"

"Well, yeah, she has to have a name, and I liked that one. According to dog breath, we will arrive at our final destination shortly. He isn't sure who you are, though. You should inform him who your dad is the moment he comes back to check on us, save your ass, and get the hell out of here."

"REALY, you don't think much of me, do you? At what point have I left you yet? And why would you think this would be any different?"

"AvX, it's because of all you have done for me that I want you to save yourself. These guys are going to take me no matter what you do, and there is no reason for you to get yourself killed in the process. I'm no one with nowhere to go. I feel like a stray someone dropped off on the highway that keeps running after the cars, hoping someone will stop and pick me up."

"Foolish little female, where is all your fire now?"

"I'm tired, AvX, and I don't mean physically. I'm not supposed to be here. I should never have survived that attack in the first place. Even though I have been nothing but a pain in the ass to you, I'm glad I got to meet my very own Smurf."

"I'm a Valerian, not a Smurf. What is this thing you keep calling me?"

I point down at the pants I have on. "See, besides the hat, you look just like them, but you are being very un-smurfy right now."

"I look nothing like these…things."

"Of course you do. Well, ok, maybe you're slightly different, but you both are blue. In the cartoon, one of them has the cutest heart tattoo. You just have lots more, especially when they light up, which is totally cool, by the way. Now muscle definition, ok I'll give you that one, you have them slightly beat in that category, but I'm not going to swell your head any bigger; you already know you have a rocking body. All you need is a surfboard, and I would be drooling all over the place. Girls at home would have been lined up on the beach just to watch this bod of yours."

"Do your Smurfs have one of these boards?"

"Absosmurfly they do."

I can't help but turn in her arms as I can feel her mischievousness. I reach up without thinking and pull her lips to mine. The shock that goes through me with that first touch is stunning. I immediately want more as I wrap an arm around her side, pulling her closer. I slide my lips over hers gently, only to be rewarded with a sigh right before she melts against me. I can't stop the moan that leaves me when she opens her mouth and I'm able to slip my tongue in, devouring the exotic taste that is Ivy's alone. Feeling her attraction towards me simply makes me squeeze her tighter, momentarily forgetting where we are until I hear footsteps coming our way. I pull away from her reluctantly, only for her to say.

"That was Smurftastic."

I am basking in the desire I feel from her when the door opens and in walks their leader.

"Valerian, I see you are back on the land of the living. I have put a few feelers out about you with no response yet. It seems your kind are rarely seen in this area. With a little information, your stay with us could be improved. There is even the possibility of talking me into letting you keep the female until we arrive at her destination. All I need to know is who you are."

"Who are you?"

"I'm known as Lurín."

"What are you planning on doing with us?"

"She is already bought and paid for; you I'm still working on." He motions for someone behind him and another of his kind brings in a tray of food.

"I will pay you double what they have offered if you let us go, no questions asked." I start to turn my wrist over to show him my father's house mark, only to hesitate.

"That amount is substantial, Valerian. The female has the highest bounty ever offered for an off-worlder. If I don't take her in, another will. Your fee to me would only keep her from their clutches for a short time. It's best to simply let the fates have her. She is insignificant in this conversation anyway, as I am a male of my word and her future is already settled. If you value your freedom and would like your ship returned, you need to be concerned about yourself from this moment on. I have added a few medical supplies to your food tray. Enjoy the female while you can, for this will be her last rising. Once we dispose of her, it will be your turn. For your sake, you better hope I stay in a good mood."

"I will not let you take her back to them to be destroyed."

"You behave as if you have a choice. Even if you managed to overpower me and get out of this room, in your weakened state, you still have an entire crew to defeat with no weapons. Your ship is even unresponsive. I advise you to come to terms with your circumstances."

He walks out of the door, and I feel Ivy trembling behind me. Her mind is once again blank as she fights her emotions. I turn in her arms and grab her face. "Look at me Ivy." I shake her lightly. "Ivy!"

She blinks a few times and I feel her erratic emotions. "Please, kill me."

Those three words practically tear my heart out.

She pushes me away and stands on wobbly legs. She has bruises all over her arms and is limping as she heads toward the food tray. "We need to get you fixed. You can't fight them in the shape you are in now. You have to survive, AvX. My sacrifice has to be for something."

I start to get up and she motions for me to stay. Tears are running down her cheeks as she gathers things in her hands. Ivy comes back, dumping everything on the floor beside me. Talking to herself as she opens a few packages. I lay still as she wipes the blood off my stomach before applying bandages I don't truly require, as I can see my wounds healing. However, right now, she needs to focus on something besides what she believes is coming for her.

Every time I start to say something, she holds her hand up and shakes her head no. She is slowly swirling into madness right in front of me, and I don't know how to stop it. I finally grab her and pull her up on top of me. She fights me at first, then settles down as I rub her back. "Ivy, calm yourself. This rising isn't over."

"Let me up, AvX. I'll tell them if you won't."

"Do you trust me?"

It takes her a moment to answer.

"I suppose."

"Close your eyes then and try to quiet your mind. I will get us out of here, and when I do, I need your fire, not your despair." I send as much peace and comfort as I can her way. She finally quits trembling and I feel her finger tracing the ruins on my chest.

"Why do they glow like this? It seems like when I move my hand away, the color fades."

"They are called runes. I get them and my size from my father, although I'm still the shortest of all my brothers."

"Do you come from a large family? I was an only child."

"I have twenty-one brothers."

"No way, your poor mother. I can't imagine having twenty-plus kids."

Laughing, I shake my head. "I bet she couldn't either, as I'm her only one."

"Oh, so your dad is one of those, huh? Just jumps from one bed to another, and up till this point, the way you talked about him. I thought he was one of the good guys."

"I have looked up to my father and my older brothers my whole life and I don't mean just because of their intense heights, either. I forget that you know nothing of our world or our cultures. I have a feeling you're going to be shocked by many things. Father, as a Commander, he has many responsibilities and demands put upon him. The males who have accepted this position have a responsibility to help the planets in their regions repopulate as birth rates are low. Their sperm is put in a lottery of sorts and the women bid according to their status. If won, the female and child are marked and taken care of for life.

"My father helped raise every one of us, though. He refused to simply donate his sperm as required and never have any further contact with his children. He actually raised his first three sons himself as circumstances removed their mothers. My own mother has nothing but high regard for him. Even though she never spoke the words to me, I believe she was secretly in love with him. Her heart would race and she blushed constantly if he was around when I was younger.

"Then one rising, I ran into her bedroom, only to see her staring at a wall with tears in her eyes. Whatever vision she had then changed her somehow and the next time she talked to Father I could feel her sadness. I asked her why she felt sad and she kissed my cheek and said *the dreams of youth are the regrets of maturity and what I always dreamed secretly would happen will never be, as his heart lay elsewhere.*

"Father trained all of us in hand to hand combat personally. He was very particular about our chosen weapons, and once we became of age, we were all given the best of education. I'm the only male he has that is not currently in some sort of battalion, or general, and that's for two reasons. First is my mother. Father doesn't stand a chance when she gets riled up. And second, my skills are best used in the background. Father and my big brother SoL like for me to help them with extremely important interrogations. I also represent Father in the meetings of the Elite. It's easy for me to determine the outcomes and feelings going around the room and to react accordingly. Father tends to react before thinking and he hates meetings. He is definitely a hands-on male. Give him a sword and a battle and he is right at home. Put him in a meeting and you will quickly be trying to find a way to get whatever the issue was settled. Then push him out of the room because he can and will argue with the best of them."

Ivy looks up at me. "Wow, a lottery. I mean, ok whatever. I have seen people waste their money on worse. What if one of the mothers was mean to the kid?"

"There are strict screenings, but I think they would be terrified of getting on Father's bad side. You will know what I'm talking about when you meet him."

She hits me on the chest. "Stop saying things like that! I'm not going to meet him, AvX. I appreciate you trying to get my mind off what's coming, but I'm not stupid. I'll be dead before your sun rises again. Even if I'm not, then what? What will happen if I do survive? I don't even know if I care anymore."

Her heart hits her chest hard, and I can tell she is barely holding on. She is fighting the urge to panic. I won't promise her anything else because she thinks I'm simply doing it to give her hope. I would love to tell her that she is the reason my runes are dancing under her fingertips, but I won't, not right now. Instead, I remain quiet, simply enjoying her laying up against me. I close my eyes and reach out around me.

It takes me a moment to push past the emotions on the ship and look further. Not many of my kind can push their emotions as well as retrieve them. I search for another and I smile when I feel the simmering rage of a familiar mind approaching.

CHAPTER 16

A vX

SHOUTS and the sound of multiple feet running makes Ivy jerk in my arms. She jumps to her feet, backing up against the wall. I have to push her panic away so that I can concentrate on father as he makes his way to us.

"Are we there already?" Ivy whispered.

It takes me a second to get to my feet, and when I do, I sway from the intense pain in my head where they hit me. Voices yell out in agony as a roar echoes through the hallway. Ivy grabs me around the waist, tucking herself into my side.

"We have to get you out of here."

She is trying to push me closer to the door when it suddenly opens. Lurín walks in first, but not as arrogant as he was before. My father has his massive arm wrapped around his neck and a knife already pressed through his cheek. Bits and pieces of blood and fur cover him. I hear Ivy mumble.

"Dearest god, let him be one of the good guys."

"AvX, son, I can see their hospitality has been lacking."

"Currency will do that, father. Do you need my assistance?"

"No, Tordan has secured all the others. They growl a lot but are easily subdued. Take the female and head back toward the ship. I believe your jailers need a private introduction and a lesson needs to be sent out about what happens to the ones who mess with my family."

Lurín jerked in father's arms. "I had no idea he was your son. He never once said anything, and I asked him multiple times."

"Your ignorance will not save you from your sins. This female needed protection, but all you saw was her worth in credits. If this had been one of your females, how would you react? She is only one of a handful left of her entire race, but you were too stupid and blinded by the prospect of sudden wealth to look into it any further. Now, because of your foolishness, you have lost the lives of your crew and yourself in the process. AvX, humor me for a moment and tell me, why did you not inform him of your status?"

"Father, I offered to buy her from him, and he refused. I knew even if I gave him the credits, she would still be sold off and I would be ejected into space. What his kind forgets is that I can feel everything he thinks, and I knew his intentions before he ever stepped into the room."

"Fair enough. See to yourself and the female. I will be along shortly."

I pull Ivy close as we start to leave the room. "Close your eyes. You don't need to see the mess dad has made of this place." She tucks her head into my side and we slowly make our way back towards the port where the Traveler is connected to their main ship.

Tordan greets me at the junction. "AvX, I see that you may need to be patched up?"

I hear Ivy gasp when she looks up at him.

"Hello, miss, my name is Tordan, and it's a pleasure. I believe your friend the AllTarra will be pleased to see you."

"Ugh, hi."

She starts trembling when she sees the tube we have to walk across. I don't even think about my injuries. I simply reach down and pick her up, expecting her to fight and try to get down, but to my relief, she throws her arms around my neck and pushes her head against my neck. Her emotions are all over the place and it breaks my heart to feel her suffering.

I can hear the AllTarra screeching throughout the ship. Walking quickly, I head straight for the medical chamber. Tordan is only steps behind me. The moment we approach the door it opens, and the AllTarra flashes her wings at us aggressively.

Tordan immediately places himself in front of us. I lower Ivy down and the moment her feet touch the floor, she darts around Tordan, opening her arms. The enormous bird settles the moment she could see her and glides effortlessly up to her, settling upon Ivy's shoulder. Her large wing curls around Ivy's back while she rubs her beak against her cheek lovingly.

Tordan stands back, a smile on his face. "I do believe I have witnessed everything now. When we arrived, I heard her screeching and was concerned how we were going to contain her. Apparently, she has attached herself to your human. I have never seen them do anything like this before. They are usually solitary creatures."

"She calls her Tarra, and as you can see, she is very protective of Ivy."

A familiar voice echoes through the room, startling me. "Oh AvX, please forgive me for putting you and Mistress Ivy in such perils."

"ANDI! It is good to hear your back with us."

Tordan walks past Ivy as she talks soothingly to Tarra and over to one of the drawers. "Come here, AvX, let's get you fixed up before your father returns."

"He does like to make an entrance doesn't he?'"

"You know your father. The moment he finds out one of his is in trouble, I don't believe anything short of death could stop him."

"You act like you are any different. I'm sure he didn't have to ask you twice."

He smiles and shrugs. "Someone has to be able to rein him in when he gets started."

Ivy turns, looking at me, then at Tordan. I try to see him the way she would and no wonder her emotions are unsettled. He is a massive male, and his cybernetics give him a brutal appearance. She takes a step forward when the door opens and father walks in with a huge grin on his face.

"I believe this was exactly what I needed. Nothing like a good fight to wake the old bones back up. AvX, my boy, I hate that you were put in this situation, but I believe you did this to yourself. Flying out during a solar storm to go shopping. You acted like a youngling heading off alone, but what's done is done, as my Kira would say."

"Father, this is Ivy."

Before he can say anything to her, ANDI's holo form appears in front of us. "Commander DaR, I am disconnecting from the other ship as we speak. SAGE just contacted me and said SiN is taunting Mistress Kira at the main dwelling. She has sent word to RaZ and XuL, they are en route."

Father and Tordan both run from the room. I start to follow them, only to turn back to Ivy first. "I'll return as quick as I can."

She motions for me to go on, but I can feel her pulling away from me.

Tordan is yelling out commands while Father paces back and forth, his Symbots moving up and down his arms.

"ANDI, how quickly can we get there?"

"Master Tordan, I have never attained jump status, but the Traveler has the appropriate engineering to achieve it. If these flares would give me only a few more moments."

SCOUT appears in his holo form. "Strap yourselves in. I only have seconds to get this right. AvX, secure the female."

I run from the room and Ivy screams when I burst through the door. Grabbing a set of restraints from the wall, I tie her to me quickly. The ship starts to shake violently and Tarra squawks as I pull her and Ivy into my arms, holding them as it feels like my skin is being stretched.

CHAPTER 17

K ira

Ickis is chasing one of his little ones around and I laugh at their antics as I pull the last of the weeds out around this new bed. Out of all the designs, for some reason this one here in the corner has become the hardest to keep up with.

"Kira, there is no reason for you to be crawling on the ground. I can have the planter bots handle that for you."

"I know that SAGE, but I enjoy doing it myself. If I allowed it, you would have those crazy ass bots pack me from room to room."

Ivy

I DON'T KNOW who is holding whom at this point, but I am sick of all this shit. The pressure against my body is so heavy I feel like my skin is being stretched. The experience isn't painful, just unnerving, and my nerves are shot. I start struggling in AvX's arms, as I feel like I'm starting to smother. He pulls me in tighter and Tarra pecks at him. As I know, she has to feel like we're crushing her in between us.

As soon as it started, it was over. I fight the restraints AvX put around us and would have fallen to the floor if he hadn't grabbed me.

My hair suddenly stands up on the back of my neck, and I know something is wrong. The Symbots flair out and up my arms as I get up. Then I feel SAGE's protective bubble settle over me a mere second before he floats out of the darkened corner I was just in. My heart hits my chest, but I refuse to cower in front of him. SiN looks so much like DaR it's disturbing, but there is no hiding the madness in his eyes.

"So we meet again. You would think that Father would have learned his lesson by now, but no, he just keeps making the same mistakes over and over."

"I'm not alone, and you can't touch me in this protective bubble."

He hits the bubble in his mist form, and I scream as I step back.

He laughs at my reaction. "Scared ya, didn't I?"

"Why are you doing this?"

"Why, why; always the same questions. I do enjoy seeing your confusion. Daddy dearest has never told you the story of how I came to be, has he? You don't need to answer that, I can tell."

"If you hate him so badly, then why not confront him?"

"What's the fun in that? You see, pretty Kira, he holds you above all others. Even though he loves his other spawns of nobleness. You hold his soul in the palm of your hand, and I want to personally watch him crumble when I take you from him."

"He would hunt you until his last breath."

"Destroying you would be his last breath, but don't fret about it too much. I would make sure you had those last moments together. I want you to fade in his arms as I watch laughing."

"You think your brothers would simply let it go after that, and that you would walk off happily ever after? You would need eyes in the back of your head for the rest of your existence."

"They haven't caught me yet, and I have been here under their nose for risings now. Their feeble attempts mean nothing to me. The only one I have to keep my eye on is the youngling human male. If he becomes too much of a risk, I will simply have to have him eliminated. Their easily damaged flesh doesn't have a chance in our world."

He walks around me, running his misty fingers over the bubble. I see Ickis standing behind him, simply waiting for him to make a move closer towards me. The bad thing about the bubble is that Ickis can't get to me either as it blocks anything that it didn't originally cover.

"SiN, what can we do to make this right? This anger, or revenge, you are holding onto is poisoning your soul. Let us help you. You haven't done anything yet that can't be forgiven. Give your father a chance, put this vendetta of yours aside."

RaZ lands on the wall, his large wings stretched out behind him as his eyes taking in the screen in front of him. Seconds later, XuL vaults over the gardens enclosure. SiN turns from me, floating effortlessly above the ground.

"Oh, the chosen ones have decided to become the heroes once again."

RaZ jumps off the wall and casually walks forward. "You really are doing your best to get his attention, aren't you?"

"I have held it for quite some time now, dear brother."

"I'm not your brother."

"On the contrary, you are, can't deny the blood. You most of all should understand the power of blood better than anyone else here."

XuL growls as both boys maneuver SiN away from me. "If you don't want to forfeit your own soul, I would advise you to never return here again."

"Good advice, but no can do. You see, our precious daddy will rue the rising he walked away from my mother. I will bring this family to its knees and I will laugh the day you beg,… **me** to stop."

RaZ and XuL both rush him at the same time, only for him to disappear right before our eyes. The only sound is his laughter fading away. RaZ takes off over the wall chasing the mist into the dark forest. XuL jumps on top of the wall, watching but refuses to leave me.

The bubble pops and Ickis rushes up my body, rubbing his face against my cheek like he is apologizing for not being right with me. "I'm fine sweetie, you shouldn't have to be on guard at your own home. SAGE, how did he manage to get in the garden? I thought your sensors would pick him up?"

"Kira, I have no idea how he is blocking his essence, but even with me seeing and hearing him, I still couldn't detect him. I am going to have to discuss guard bots with Master DaR. I can't protect you from something I can't see."

XuL jumps off the wall and comes over to me. I'm trying to act brave, but he can see right through it. Ickis is curled all around me, but when XuL opens his arms, I walk into them, hug him back tightly. There is no hiding the tremors wracking my body.

"I came as quickly as my legs would carry me. I'm sorry we failed you, Kira."

"Oh, stop it." I step back away from him. "I'm still here, so you did your job. I refuse to be scared in my own home. That boy has some serious issues, and I believe your father owes all of us an explanation. I have waited patiently for him to tell me, but no longer."

"Grab your stuff. I had to give Brittany the look in order for her to stay behind and now I will need to grovel to keep from sleeping on the couch. Thank the fates the younglings were still practicing. The only one who saw me leaving was Raven."

"What about RaZ? Should you go with him?"

"He will report back if he finds anything. We know not to take on SiN alone and also Father has called dibs. I would love to figure out how he is staying hidden. Father worries me that he has allowed this to go on for so long. I believe he thinks if the male would simply give him the chance, he could talk some sense into him, but I can see the crazy in SiN's eyes. There is no redeeming him. Father is going to underestimate his powers and regret it, I fear."

"You and me both, dear."

SAGE's voice startles me out of my thoughts. "Kira, XuL… the Traveler will dock with Falcor shortly."

"How is that possible? Did he reach AvX quicker than you thought?"

"No Kira, they did an experimental space jump in order to get here as quickly as possible. They are lucky they didn't end up vaporized in that short of a distance."

"I'm gonna ring that man's neck. How dare he take those types of chances with his life? Let alone Tordan or anyone else onboard. He knows you boys would never allow anything to happen to me."

"Kira, you know that when it concerns you, Father loses all rational thoughts."

"Take it easy, you're fine."

"Don't you're fine me, dammit! I'm sick of this bullshit. I have been violated, tortured, used as a damn snack, kidnapped, sold, and now stretched. I'm over this crap. I want my feet on solid ground and I'm never getting on another ship ever again. Do you hear me?" By the time I quit screaming all that, I'm crying again. I wipe the tears off my face angrily. "So what now? I'm so damn excited I can't contain myself."

"ANDI?"

"AvX, we have arrived safely back to Falcor and will be docking momentarily. Commander DaR will be departing immediately. Would you like me to prepare you a shuttle also?"

AvX looks down at me, his bright silver eyes seeing everything. "Ivy, would you like to get cleaned up first, or would you prefer to head on toward Darverius and our home estate?"

I shrug my shoulders. "How am I supposed to know what to do, AvX? Yes, it would be nice to have some real clothes and get cleaned up, but unless you have a local Walmart or a mall, this is all I own. Once again, I'm living on your charity." I point down at the torn-up pajamas I have on.

"Stop overthinking everything. Clothing is an easy fix, as you will soon learn. I know none of the experiences you have had so far have been overly pleasant, but Falcor is a marvel of scientific wonder. I promise there will be some positives here. Nothing in this galaxy messes with him."

"Whatever, AvX, at this point, what does it matter?"

I can tell he is at a loss as to what to do with me. The loneliness practically crushes me as I stand here, realizing I have no one. AvX is only putting up with me because I was forced upon him, nothing more. Those few kisses we shared were only to comfort me. He starts to say something, and I turn away and head towards the door. I'm over *the everything will be ok* speech, it's all just empty words. Tarra lands gently on my shoulder, and her subtle weight comforts me.

The door slides open and I hear footsteps headed my way. I immediately think the worst until I see it's Tordan and AvX's father. I stop, looking at them, as they are deep in conversation. DaR, there are no words to explain his extremely terrifying masculinity, except damn he is intense and way too good looking for his own good. Tordan has a soothing voice, his hair most women would die for, but the scars all over his body show the horrors he has lived through. They are both absolutely scary, big in muscle and height.

AvX walks past me. They stop as he approaches. DaR seems preoccupied and antsy, like he is ready to leap into space if that means he could get to where he needs to be quicker. AvX's coloring is extreme compared to their grayness. His skin pulses in shimmering shades of blue as his muscles move. He is a few inches shorter in height and not as bulky as the other two, but he holds my attention more than they do.

He stands there half-naked in dark pants that hang low on his slim hips. Talking with his hands that I just noticed are tipped with short black claws. Even though we have been together for a while now, I feel like I'm seeing him for the first time. His hair is shaggy on top. Small, pointed ears poke through the sides as he moves his head around. At first, I thought his hair was solid dark blue, but now I can see that there are purple and silver streaks as well. He turns back, looking at me for a moment, and his silver eyes flash right before he smiles. Those eyes of his are mesmerizing, they seem to see everything good or bad. His jawline and cheeks are so sharp they look like someone sculpted them. He doesn't resemble DaR at all, so he must have gotten his looks from his mother.

Tarra bumps the side of my head, and I reach up, scratching her tummy through her feathers. They start to move closer and she flares her wings out. When she does this, her feathers turn hard momentarily and flash a bright, whitish blue light. This is the second time I have seen her do this, and it's almost like she is able to send out an electrical charge. I'm lucky to have always been on this side of her anger.

AvX puts his hand out. "Easy, Tarra, they don't mean you nor Ivy any harm. Are you ready to spread those wings?"

She coos prettily and I can't help but giggle at her excitement. Too bad I don't feel the same way.

A strange commanding voice echoes through the room, and I jump. "Commander DaR, your shuttle is awaiting you at shuttle bay three. General Tordan, Luna is requesting your assistance in planting bay one. AvX, I have prepared your rooms, also a nest has been provided in the botanical garden for the AllTarra."

"Thank you Falcor, we will take Tarra to her nest first."

"What do you mean, you are taking her somewhere?"

"She will be more comfortable in the garden until we can return her home."

"So, you are taking her from me?"

"No, Ivy, you can stay with her as much as you want, but she can't have the run of the ship. She may be tame with you, but with others, she could be very aggressive."

"Fine, but I won't make her go if she doesn't want to. If it causes a problem, I will simply stay there with her."

A large ramp lowers down out of the wall and they all turn walking ahead of me and down it. I stop at the top, looking around at all the other ships, only for my mind to think. *Where is the force when you need it?*

AvX must have realized I wasn't right behind him because he stops and looks back at me. This is just another normal day in their world. I'm the stray lingering in the background, wondering if I should be scared or take the chance. He reaches a hand out for me and I hesitate before I reach out and take it.

"Come on, the first step is always the hardest. Once you get cleaned up, and a good meal in your belly, you will feel like a whole new person."

The ship is enormous and there are beings, people, and aliens walking around everywhere. I cling to AvX's hand tightly, a few nod their head as we walk by, but most act like,… well, I'm not as weird to them as they are to me.

He takes a path away from the others and it seems like we make twenty turns down these long hallways. I'll never find my way around on my own. Suddenly, it's like we step into a coliseum filled with flowers and trees. Well, what I'm assuming are trees and flowers, but whatever they are, all the different colors are beautiful. The area is immense and welcoming, with paths and swings placed in different places. Tarra flies off my shoulder and I watch as she swoops, diving in and out of what I'm assuming are trees. It looks like something you would read about in a fairy tale. AvX leads me through a windy path as I look around in amazement.

"It is a marvel, isn't it?"

"It's amazing. I can't believe something like this is on a ship. Tarra will love this."

"She has already found her nest, look there." He points, showing me the largest tree I have ever seen anywhere, and there she is prancing around inside a nest the size of a small car. When she sees me standing under her. She flies down, swirling around me, her wings caressing my cheek as she circles, then turns to fly back up to her nest.

"Come on, she is fine. Let's go get cleaned up."

"Will we be far from her?"

"No, and Falcor will notify us immediately if she starts flying through the halls looking for you. I told her that we were going to rest and would return soon."

I follow behind him, never taking my eyes off Tarra until we were back in the hall. He stops just a short distance away in front of a door. "This is you. I'm right across the hall. Everything you need should already be in there."

I pull away from him, fighting the tears that are pooling behind my eyes. "So this is it, huh? Thanks for saving my life and all that stuff. I reckon I'll see you around, maybe." When I start to turn, he grabs my arm.

"Hey, I'm just going to be across the hall, not amongst the cosmos. You have a bad habit of pushing the ones who are trying to care about you away. I'm not going anywhere, so stop shoving and go on. I will be right across the hall and the door will be open if you need me. I'll come to check on you in half a rising."

I bite the inside of my lip and simply turn away. The door magically opens and I step inside. It practically hits me in the butt as it closes quickly behind me. Shockingly, the room looks like something you would see in a magazine on Earth. There is a burgundy couch with flowered pillows and a large chair in one corner. A massive four-poster bed sits against the wall in the other one and is decorated in a lighter shade. I walk forward, amazed at how earthly it all looks and even smells. If I hadn't been through the depths of hell here lately, I would think I had walked into an expensive hotel. A light comes on through a door to my left and I look around a corner. There is an enormous tub sitting in the middle of a luxurious bathroom.

"Mistress Ivy, would you prefer a bath or a shower?"

A small girl appears out of nowhere and I jump back, screeching. "Son of a bitch, what is it with people appearing and disappearing around here? Ever heard of knocking on the door? Damn, **I want to go home**!"

"There is no cause for alarm, Ivy. You will become accustomed to me popping in and out. Alana is preparing some clothing for you now and Luna will be down to talk to you once you have rested. Oh, where are my manners? I'm SAGE, by the way. I do a little bit of everything around here and also on Darverius. I know things have been intense for you and I'm sure you have lots of questions, but all will be revealed in time. Right now, it's time to relax a little and get settled. I promise we will become great friends. Now, how about that bath? Mistress Kira swears a good bath fixes just about everything."

I run my hand through her flickering form.

"That tickles, behave. I am pleased to see you are healed and seem to be in good spirits, unlike the last time I saw you."

"I don't remember seeing you before."

"I helped ANDI and Master AvX come up with a way to heal you, but that was risings past, and this is now. We can never surrender to the flow of time, just have to keep pushing on. The bath water is ready whenever you are. There are soaps and shampoos on the side table. I will give you some privacy. Just yell out when you're done."

She disappears again. I walk over to the tub and run my fingers through the hot water. When I start to take my shirt off, I look up, seeing myself in the mirror. Who in the hell is that degenerate-looking thing? My hair is knotted and sticking up all over. There are huge bags under my eyes, and I look like I have a bad sunburn. My arms are lined with bruises and minor cuts. I take my clothes off only to find more of the same all over me. Climbing into the tub, I wince as the water burns my skin slightly.

I lay down submerged clear to my neck and let out a tense sigh. The room is eerily quiet. This is not a good thing because it gives me time to think about what has happened to me. I keep seeing mom's face and hearing her voice in my head. The water starts to swirl around me and I shake off the melancholy, determined to get these knots out of my hair.

I lay in the tub until I look like a prune. When I start to get up, a towel simply appears and I refuse to dwell on the how. As I'm wrapping it around me, SAGE pops back in.

"I figured you were about done. Let's get you over to the vanity and let me show you some neat little tricks me and Kira have devised."

"Who is Kira? I have heard her name several times now."

"She is my best friend and the first of your kind found...more importantly she is DaR's mate."

"Ughh, he is intense."

"No truer words said."

I can't help but smile at her facial expressions. "Do you change forms depending on who or what you are around? I'm sorry, I'm not sure what you are?"

"I had that option at one time, but this is my chosen holo form. I admired Kira and the others so much that it was an easy pick for me. Personally, I don't believe there is another race as beautiful as yours, so I took the best of each and here I am." She twirls around, then curtseys. "ANDI, he is the same type of AI I am, but you haven't met SCOUT yet. Whoooo, that AI will get the heart beating, as he is quite intimidating, but I have him wrapped around my little finger, he just won't admit it.

"Now let's get these knots out of your hair and some moisturizer on your tender skin, then off to bed for you. No visitors, until you have rested."

CHAPTER 19

I^{vy}

THE SOUND of someone walking around the room wakes me up. It takes me a second to remember where I am as I was asleep before my head hit the pillow.

"Hello, sleepy head, I'm sorry I woke you up. I was trying to put all this away without waking you."

I pull the covers up under my neck and scoot back when she plops down on the side of the bed. "I'm Alana, by the way, I brought you some clothes."

"You're human?"

"Last time I checked, yeah. I have a few extras now, but for the most part I am still all Earth girl. AvX had me come in and check on you. I found him pacing the hallway outside your room."

"Why didn't he come on in?"

"You will have to ask him that. I think he was trying to give you some space. Ha, space I made a funny,…but you're not laughing. If it makes you feel any better and it won't, you are not the only one of us that questioned the, WHY ME! Out of all the girls on Earth, you are not the only one who lost everything either. We all have been through one type of hell or another, but us Earth girls are tough and since you're lying here in front of me, you made it. You need to concentrate on that and not waste another minute looking back. There is nothing but darkness back there. Head towards the light, if you know what I mean."

"You make it sound so easy and you seem to have adjusted well."

"It was a process, but having the others to lean on helped. Of course, my big giant always knows how to cheer me up."

"Giant?"

"Yeah, don't let him freak you out when he comes stomping down the hall. He is loud and boisterous, but the biggest teddy bear ever. The day he found me was one of the best and worst of my life, but I would do it all again to be here with him."

Her bubbly attitude just pisses me off. "Ok, you are probably not going to like what I have to say as you seem to be attached to yours, but what is this, the new norm, or a requirement? An alien guy finds a human girl and they just hook up? I mean, it looks like you all have just got cozy with the locals. I'm not going to be anyone's broodmare or arm candy. This is a nightmare I'm still wanting to wake up from. AvX is great and all, but he is gonna run like hell as soon as he pawns me off on someone else. Should I start an alien application process and see who applies for an emotionally distressed human girl?"

She stands up and walks over, folding some of the clothes she brought in. "I have come to love my local, as you call them. I'm older than you and in all my years on Earth, I never found anyone to care for me the way SoL does. You're mad and angry at the circumstances. We all were. But I can warn you that alienating yourself from the rest of us, or the locals, won't take you back home. Dwelling on the past just makes you bitter. You need to come to terms that this is now your home, and these locals are all the family you will ever have. AvX is a gentle soul and from what I can tell, you are his exact opposite. If this is how you plan on proceeding, then maybe you should tell him to waste his affections on someone who will look past where he is from and his differences."

"He doesn't want me. I was thrust upon him."

"You are showing your age, Ivy. A piece of advice when it comes to the locals. A soul knows when it's with who it's been searching for. Don't throw their feelings and emotions back at them because it isn't the same as yours. They are alien, they have attachments and insights we don't, but it doesn't make their feelings less. If that gentle soul pacing the hallway right now cares about you and you push him away. Then you deserve the bitterness that is eating you alive. Now if you will excuse me, my local is probably wondering what's taking me so long, and I hope your clothes fit."

I start to apologize, but she is out of the door before I can say a word. I see a flash of blue skin as the door closes back. I crawl out of the bed and head towards the clothing she had laid on a side table. Happy to see several pieces of everything. I grab a pair of panties and then the softest leggings I have ever felt. I rummage around looking for a bra, but there aren't any. I finally grab one of the shirts and tug it down over my butt. Running my fingers through my hair, I head for the door. AvX is walking off just as it opens. He must hear it because he turns back.

"Hi."

CHAPTER 20

A vX

THE SOUND of her door sliding open stops me in my tracks. I turn just as she sticks her head out. She says something, and it takes me a minute to respond. I have looked at her, but I don't think I saw her until now. Long sun-colored hair flows almost to her waist in long waves. Bright grayish blue eyes peer out at me with a questioning look on her face. Her cheeks are flushed, but the redness has left her skin and now she looks young and vibrant. She is stunning, even with that constant frown of hers.

I walk back towards her without even noticing I moved. I stand before her and even though I'm not as tall as my brothers. I have to look down at her because she is so small, she only comes to my shoulders, the perfect height to tuck into my side. I reach out, running my claws through her long hair. "How are you feeling? You look breathtaking!"

She looks away and I can tell she doesn't believe me. I reach a finger up under her chin, making her look up at me as I run a finger across her cheek. "You are practically glowing, Ivy. Looks like all you needed was some rest. Someone has been squawking for you all rising. You feel like getting out for a little bit?"

She shakes her head yes. "I need shoes. Hang on, I'm sure she brought some."

Moments later, she is back. "I'm ready."

I reach my hand out, and hesitantly she takes it. The ruins on that arm light up when our skin touches. She traces the one on my hand with her fingers but doesn't say a word. Her feelings are oddly quiet right now. "You ok?"

Shrugging, she looks up at me. "I have a lot on my mind, is all. Thank you for, well, thanks. Let's go see Tarra before she comes to find us."

We can hear her before we ever get to the conservatory. "Someone is making a fuss this morning." The moment Tarra sees us, she swoops down, landing gently on Ivy's shoulder.

"Hey, pretty girl, what's wrong, don't you like your nest?"

She coos and then stretches her wings out wide before shaking her feathers all over.

"Actually, I think she knows she is close to home."

"What do you mean?"

"Darverius, that's where the rest of her kind are located."

"Is that right, pretty girl, you wanna go home?"

The AllTarra tucks her head into Ivy's hair, making little clicking noises.

"I don't want her unhappy, and I know no matter how pretty the cage is. This room is still a cage. Can we take her home?"

"We can, but that means getting on a ship."

"How did I know you were going to say that?"

"The positive thing is, it's a quick trip. You will get to meet the other females and Tarra can easily fly from the dark forest to where we would be staying."

She hesitates to ask me something. "You are going to stay with me?"

"Ivy, I have no place I would rather be, even though you don't believe me."

"It's not you AvX… it's all of this. You have been nothing but kind to me, and …well, shit. I'm not good at acting thankful. I know my own faults, believe me. Even standing right next to you, I feel alone and I don't know how to deal with that. I've always been a handful, and it's not like I do that deliberately. I don't know how to shut off the fight-or-flight mode I seem to be installed with. When you look at me, what do you see?"

I pull her trembling form over and put my arms around her. Tarra coos as she also enjoys the attention. "Ivy, you are not ready for me to tell you what I see when I look at you. One rising you will awaken and the fight will no longer be needed as your heart won't feel so heavy. I think you are pushing yourself too hard. No one expects you to be ok with your situation, but I do need you to be more open-minded. You ready for your next adventure?"

She sighs and I can feel her breath against my skin. I don't think she even realizes how tightly she is holding onto me. I kiss the top of her forehead and smile when I think about how many times I have watched father do the same thing to comfort his little human. They need touch as much, if not more, than we do. My little human is in fight mode, and I'm not sure what needs to be done for her to see the world around her in a more positive way. "Come, I'll have Falcor get the shuttle ready and you can grab a bag to put some of your new clothes in."

"Can I take Tarra with me?"

"Falcor, is it ok for Ivy to take the AllTarra with her until our departure?"

"If that bird poops anywhere on my decks, I will have her served for last meal."

Tarra shrieks out, insulted. I swear the feelings coming from her make me believe she understands more than we think.

We walk back down the hall. "I will meet you back here in a few minutes." For once she is standing in the hall waiting for me first. She has a small bag over one shoulder while Tarra coos on the other one. As we approach the shuttle bay, I see her slow down with all the activity in the room.

"Wow, would you look at that view? It looks like we could just step outside."

"Well, don't try it. You wouldn't last seconds. I have been told of things called rollercoasters in your world. Do you know of these?"

"Absolutely. I always was an adrenaline junkie."

"You will love this, then. Come on, let me get you and Tarra settled."

"You're not going to put her in a cage?"

"Nope, she says she would rather stay with you. Don't be shocked if she scratches you accidentally, though. The first drop can take your breath."

I take the seat in front of her and lower the hatch down. "Falcor, we are ready when you are." The shuttle moves up and out towards the dock. I have done this so many times I could probably sleep through it, but I'm interested in how Ivy is going to react.

We launch out of the main dock and the shuttle seems to hover in place for less than the blink of an eye before the nose dips and we shoot down towards Darverius. Ivy lets out a scream behind me. "Hold your arms up, AvX!" She is smiling as she screams out playfully.

This is the first genuine smile I have ever seen on her face, and I'm immediately enchanted. This is my new goal. I plan on seeing that happiness and carefree smile on her face often. I feel myself smiling back, enjoying the intense joy she is projecting.

We break through the planet's atmosphere, and she starts laughing. "We so have to do that again, but next time without Tarra. I don't think she enjoyed it as much as I did."

"We will land shortly. Take a look out the viewer and tell me what is the biggest difference between your homeworld and mine."

"Wow, would you look at all those colors? Earth has more neutral tones, blue oceans, green forests, and concrete cities. But it's those hidden places that just rock your world when you find them. It's like, I took a hiking trip once with Tommy and we came upon a place where the creek bed turned suddenly and all the water disappeared into the side of the hill. The place was so pretty and just lush and green. There were dragonflies and water skippers playing above the water everywhere. I remember thinking how magical the place was. I went back to that place many times by myself when I was trying to escape. I reckon when I think about it, I have always been running away from something."

"I would have loved to have seen that. I have several places like that on my mother's planet. Hopefully, one rising, I will be able to show them to you. Was this Tommy a close friend?"

I feel her sadness once again and I regret asking her about him.

"We grew up together. He is who I was with when I was taken. I cared about him, but I no longer was infatuated with him like I was when we were kids. Tommy was a great guy and would have been a good husband for some lucky girl, just not me. I was simply using him to escape. We had worked hard to save up enough to leave home. I refused to listen and was determined to make something out of myself. I was convinced that all I had to do was get out of that town and everything would fall into place. I was gonna prove them all wrong. Even if I hadn't been taken, abducted, whatever you want to call it. I was dead the moment I got in that car with him. I reckon when I say it out loud like that. I should be grateful for,... well, that I'm here in this flying pencil with you."

She gets quiet again, and I can tell she was finally hearing her own words. "Hold Tarra, we are getting ready to land in front of my father's main dwelling. I'm going to warn you upfront. Several of my brothers are here with their families. Before they steal you from me, we will see what Tarra is going to do first."

We land lightly and the hatch pulls back. I jump out, then grab Ivy by the waist, lowering her down to the ground. She smiles up at me, and I can feel her attraction as she straightens her shirt.

Tarra squawks loudly. Ivy reaches up, scratching her under her beak.

"Ok, pretty girl, I get it; let's get a move on. Miss thing is in a hurry, AvX, so lead the way. What's the rush, pretty girl? You got a hot date?"

I can't help but laugh at Ivy. This is a side of her I could get used to quickly. She starts to walk away and I can't help but notice how those leggings she has on hugs her butt cheeks. My ruins flare, giving my thoughts away. I'm safe right now because she doesn't understand that they are responding to her. I will find a way to make her mine. She simply doesn't realize that I'm chipping slowly away at that wall she has up all around her.

CHAPTER 21

I^{vy}

WE WALK AWAY from the shuttle and what appears to be an absolutely enormous house. I can hear others talking, but instead of us heading inside, AvX turns and we walk out towards a field. For some reason I can't seem to keep my eyes off him today. The odd double suns shining down upon us is making his skin glisten and shimmer with every movement. His tight black pants hug every inch of the muscles in his powerful legs. A dark gray vest hangs loosely on his shoulders, and tempts me with a flash of skin every time he moves. He reaches over, taking my hand in his, and his runes light up. All they are doing is making me want to strip him down and see what other parts of his body are lined in these bright swirls. I swear, the more I look at him, the prettier he gets. He smiles down at me, his eyes flashing a stunning silver, and I look away, knowing I have been caught ogling him. Tarra prances impatiently on my shoulder as we walk across a wide field.

"Where are we headed?"

"You will see."

I am so busy looking around, amazed at how different, but the same everything is. I almost jump out of my skin when Tarra shrieks loudly and launches off my shoulder. Her large wing brushes past my face as she goes. I pull back, stopping me and AvX both at the sight before me. All this time we have been walking in what I would call an odd type of wheat field, but the darkness of what appears to be almost another world radiates warning the closer we get. Even the two suns above can't seem to penetrate the eeriness that immediately makes me want to turn away.

"What is this place? Do we have to go in there?"

"This is the dark forest. Its vastness separates one part of the continent from the other. My brother RaZ and his wife Katherine live practically in the middle. I figure it's a good way to keep from having much company. His pets, the Selin, are quite terrifying, not only in mass, but they have row after row of teeth. You will meet SeeSee, my Keida's Selin protector, shortly. You wouldn't think this with her personality, but Tarra's kind flourishes in the darkness of its mass interior. We believe that's the reason their feathers light up. The dark forest houses many animals that thrive in darkness only. If the AllTarra feels threatened, the flash of light from their feathers blind and terrifies most animals."

I watch Tarra hesitate to enter into it. She keeps circling above me and then back again. Another shriek has her turning when an AllTarra twice her size emerges out of the darkness and straight towards her.

I put my hand over my mouth, terrified that the larger animal will hurt my Tarra, but they simply fly around each other. The larger one sweeps down, barely missing us, and I hear Tarra let out an aggressive sound.

"What's happening? Should I yell for her to come back?"

"It's a male. He must have heard her calling out. He is warning us off, but she let him know real fast that we were her family."

I raise my arm up and she lands softly, only to look back up at the other huge AllTarra circling us. A growl unlike anything I have ever heard sounds behind us and I swear I almost pee on myself when I turn, seeing the creature, or should I say the teeth, standing practically right on top of us.

I start trembling all over, but before I can run or even react. Tarra flies off my arm and right towards the massive hound, her wings flashing bright and aggressively. The beast turns away, whining as it heads back into the darkness. Only when it has disappeared completely does Tarra head back up into the sky.

AvX pulls me close and I tuck my head into his chest, enjoying the safety I only seem to feel in his arms. This is the first time I have noticed he smells like bubblegum.

"It's ok, she scared him off."

"What in the Sam hell was that thing?"

"That was one of the Selin I was just telling you about. They are the main protectors of the dark forest and RaZ's faithful companions. He was probably patrolling the area, and we were too close to its border. Now that I think about it, our family has several very unlikely animals as pets. No different from your attachment to Tarra. If she had been born in the wild, she would have attacked you, in the same manner, to keep you from her nest or her young."

The male flies close to Tarra, and she coos playfully. "Girl, you're gonna give up the goods way too easily. Make him work for it a little bit." She circles a couple more times before heading into the forest with him.

"Will she be ok?"

"AllTarra's mate for life, he has probably been waiting on her for what feels like a lifetime to him."

"Will I ever see her again?" I can feel the tears coming.

"Absolutely. She will always be able to find you. Once bonded, the AllTarra tracking capabilities are uncanny."

A gigantic form appears before us, and I scream, running behind AvX. "Shit, damn, hell, I wish people would quit doing that."

"Master AvX, forgive me for startling you, but Commander DaR is requesting your presence in the main dining chamber."

AvX is laughing as he pulls me back around him. "Tell Father we will be there shortly SCOUT."

He nods and poof; he is gone again. AvX is still laughing.

I smack him on the arm playfully. "That's not funny. It's not normal for things, people, whatever the hell, those things are to just pop up out of thin air. Can't someone put a bell around their necks or something? Maybe they could make a sound right before they appear. What if someone was bumping uglies or something? You know, some needed privacy."

"Bumping what?"

AvX is laughing so hard he is making me laugh. "You know, bumping uglies!" I point at his crotch.

"Oh, my little human, I never know what is going to come out of that mouth of yours. You are such a joy. I'm going to remember this bumping of uglies as you call it. My brothers will be as amused as I am with that term. Come, Father is not a patient male, and if he sent SCOUT to get us, it must be serious."

"Oh, damn, can we just stay here, then? I'm tired of serious bad stuff."

"I agree, Ivy. I could use some downtime myself. I'm going to warn you ahead of time that you will be overwhelmed by everyone. I was hoping to introduce you to them all a little slower, but it looks like you are going to get thrown into the mix quickly. I want you to remember one thing when we get into that room. Every male in there, including me, would and will give his life to keep you safe. The majority of them will be my brothers and even though they are a loud, colorful bunch, I am lucky to call them family. It won't be long and you will feel the same way. Come on, let's head towards the dwelling."

"That's your house?"

"Well, it is the main family's dwelling. All of us have rooms here."

"So it's your house?"

"I don't have a permanent residence anywhere, actually. I kinda jump around from here, to Falcor, then to Mother's."

"Oh, I see, a momma's boy!"

"Absolutely, won't even deny it."

CHAPTER 22

D aR

Proudly, I watch several of my sons walk into the room. The ones lucky enough to have found them hover around their mates protectively. My Kira wanders around the room, giving hugs and taking the time to talk to each one of them the way she always does. The only ones not here or on a comm unit are Keida and Danny. I had them stay later at training this rising with Zura at my request. This is a conversation I didn't feel was appropriate for the younglings.

EvO is the last to link up on the holo screen as several of my younglings couldn't make it because of the solar flares. ViN still hasn't checked in according to Falcor, so I will forward this recording to his shuttle, then make arrangements for Hugo to send a team out to see if he can be located. I'm not overly worried as I know Targres Four, especially in the desolate areas, messes with their personal comm units, and ViN is not a male many would mess with.

AvX enters into the room, his arm around the waist of the newest addition to the family. I can see the moment she enters into the room she is overwhelmed. Her eyes are big and even though she is trying to put on a brave act, she is trembling slightly. I whistle and motion for everyone to have a seat. I do this not only for her, but for myself before I chicken out, as Kira would put it.

SoL tugs Alana onto his lap, his horns wrapping around her lovingly. XuL pulls a chair out, settling Brittany. I watch as he kisses her on top of her forehead before taking the seat next to her. Tordan and Luna have remained on Falcor, but I can see the concern on their faces. Father pulls me into a hug before he takes his seat next to me on the left, along with his beauty Victoria. Apparently, I have fooled no one by saying this was a simple gathering.

RaZ and Katherine are the last to come through the door and I can't help but smile as I hear their laughter as he chases her through the hall towards us. The smile leaves his face the moment he enters the room, though. He could tell immediately that something is wrong. Katherine goes quickly to a seat next to Victoria while RaZ stands guard behind her. His large wings jerk aggressively as he looks around.

Kira walks up to me and I put my arm around her, pulling her tight before placing her in the seat to my right. She had put her foot down demanding answers after SiN made his last appearance, and I promised her I would tell her everything, but I wasn't going to say it twice. This was a part of my life I never wanted to relive, but my hand has been forced. I know some of my words will hurt Kira and this bothers me more than anything else. That's why I have put this off for so long.

"Now that you all have been seated, there is something I need to inform you of. When SiN's appearance was first brought to our attention, even though he looks just like me, I was in denial of his identity and thought it was no one's business concerning the events of my past. However, I have come to believe that I was wrong to keep this from you. Because my mate and my younglings all have the right to know how SiN came to be in existence. This story will take a moment, so please wait until I'm done to ask me any questions."

I run my hand through my hair and get up out of my chair. My ruins flash a bright red while I try to get my thoughts straight. I have said it over and over in my head, but now I'm lost on how to proceed.

"Father had been missing almost two complete Orbital rotations, and I was facing the last of my Commander trials. A goal I had worked for my entire existence up to that point. I had put off packing up the last of Father's things in Solanar until my hand was forced to do so when he was pronounced dead. Packing up his apartments was like losing him all over again. I was having a hard time dealing with all these emotions and I was distracted carrying a hoverboard down a few steps with some of his books on it. I came around a bend and accidentally bumped into someone, barely catching them before they fell down several flights of stairs.

"I can remember it like it happened last rising. The look on her face as I was holding her in my arms. I was immediately smitten with her beauty. Her name was Serena, and she was the first-born daughter of one of our remaining elders. She was way above me in ranks, but that didn't stop me from seeking her out. I was like every other young male at the time. Hot-headed and madly in love with someone I had no chance of winning, but nothing was going to keep me from trying. I used my status and my training to hack into her personal schedule. Anytime she was in a public area, I made sure to be there as well. After a while, I must have grown on her because I finally convinced her to let me court her, and I went out of my way to win her hand once I felt confident in her feelings for me. I approached her father about combining our houses. He was delightfully receptive to the idea, which shocked and pleased me at the time. My own father had been a well-known figure before he left us and, because of his high praise of me and my personal wealth, her father agreed to the match.

"I can remember practically prancing around if she was on my arm. I wanted all to know who she belonged to. I bought her jewels and lavished her with exotic gifts. There were only two downsides to our budding romance. One was her sister, Samora.

The female was in her sister's shadow constantly. It was hard to have a private moment with Serena because she was always lurking around, watching. She wasn't an ugly female, but she seemed off and would take to having fits if she wasn't provided with what she wanted. The second was my Commandership, something I had been working so hard towards my whole life. None of the previous commanders had mates, and I was going to have to choose between my career and her.

"It only took a few of her kisses and the feeling of her in my arms for me to make the choice. I purchased our mating bands, and I was going to ask her to be mine that rising. I couldn't live another moment without her in my arms. For some unknown reason, I had hesitated to take myself out of the last commandership tournament until I had her answer."

I start walking around the room, refusing to look any of them in the eye, as this is the most uncomfortable part.

"I remember being announced and when I walked into her rooms. I was so shocked at what I was seeing, I couldn't say a word. There she lay in front of me wearing barely anything at all, and when she motioned me forward, I practically tripped over my own feet to get to her. I started to say something and I can remember her shushing me then handing me a glass. I chugged that stuff down so fast that it wasn't until afterwards that I realized it tasted tainted.

"She stripped my clothes off me slowly, and I laid back, enjoying the feeling of her tight sheath surrounding my young shaft. I remember murmuring her name over and over, but then the outer door opened, and in she walked. It was like it was all happening in slow motion. My seed released inside who I thought was my mate, but then who was the female standing in the doorway with her hand over her mouth and tears in her eyes? When I glanced up at the woman who had given herself so thoroughly to me, I still saw my Serena. Until she went to laughing and the glamor she was wearing failed, showing me her true identity. It had been Samora I was making love to all along.

"I can remember throwing her off me and grabbing my pants. Serena ran from the room while Samora laughed, sprawled on the floor naked before me. The guards rushed into the room and not so gently threw me out of their dwelling. I screamed Serena's name, but even I knew there was no repairing what happened.

"No matter what I did, they wouldn't let me talk to her. Finally, on the day of my Commander's trials, she commed me before I had to leave. She said that Samora admitted to drugging me and using a glamor to conceal her identity. And even though it wasn't my fault, and that she knew I cared for her greatly, she could not overlook what had happened… that she would be haunted by that sight for eternity. Samora had been sent away and I should go on with my life. She wished me luck at the trials and that was the last I ever spoke to her.

"She left Darverius shortly afterward and mated a prince in one of the outer quadrants. They hadn't been mated long when their home was attacked and they were both killed.

"I spent many a darkness alone in my quarters wondering what could have been. Would I have always been so smitten with her, or would I have slowly come to hate her because I gave up my commandership? Would she have still been alive? The questions never stopped in the beginning. But we all know the Lord of Light always has a plan, whether we like the path or not. Each of you was meant to be here, and I was meant to be your father.

"I didn't know that I had gotten Samora pregnant until SiN made his appearance. The thought never crossed my mind as a possibility as I pushed forward, only concentrating on my career. Then the raising of my own younglings.

"Once SiN made himself known, I was able to dig up where she was sent, but the worst of it was when Tordan found his birth records. Not knowing of SiN's existence was horrible, but he was one of two. The other little one only lived a few minutes after birth. It was a girl." The entire room lets out a gasp.

"Samora had been sent away without a dime to her name. Her parents were so ashamed of the way she had conducted herself ;they marked her from their records like she had never existed. Apparently, she had no choice but to sell herself to survive, blaming me and her sister for all the things that had befallen her. From the moment SiN was born, she told him I was the reason for the pain and suffering they were going through. She taught him to hate me and when she died, he vowed to make me pay for what had been done to his mother.

"SiN has been residing on Darverius for quite some time, and I know he is staying in the dark forest somewhere. RaZ has hunted for him as have his Selin's. All that I know is that someone has to be hiding him. He has tried to take Kira several times, and he needs to be stopped. Because we know he will do anything to hurt the ones I care about. My heart hurts for the male he could have become, especially if I would have known of his existence, and for the daughter, I would have spoiled like no other."

At some time, Kira had walked up to me and had tucked herself into my side. I pull her close, needing her strength after baring my biggest SiN for all to see.

Katherine stands up. "DaR, are you sure the female died at birth?"

"That's what the records are showing, yes."

She shakes her head and everyone at the table can see her confusion. "DaR, I don't think she is dead. I mean, she is, and she isn't. All this time I knew there was something different, something wrong with Ellaria. She isn't in the in-between she is more. Now that I think about it, her eyes have always looked familiar... they're yours. I believe the princess that has haunted the dark forest for years is your daughter, DaR."

She no more says that than the entire room goes dark and out of the wall floats in a ghostly female figure. She glides in, her hair flowing wildly around her in a non-existing wind, a long white gown gracing her form. Her mouth opens, and it takes me a second for her words to be heard.

"I didn't know! All this time, I have walked, searching, and you were right here in front of me. I was drawn here as a little one and I have watched over you for orbital rotations, never knowing why. SiN is the darkness to my light. His mind is closed, and full of hate, he refuses to listen to reason. My light recognized him long ago, but he wants no part of me. You can't save him, nor me. It lightens my heart to know you are my true father, but the darkness of my mother's spirit still feeds SiN's soul. Only the one who holds the light can diminish him for good. Guard our family well,… Father."

We all watch in amazement as she brightens, then dims. Slowly the room lightens back, and she is gone. The tears flow freely from my eyes as I sink my face into Kira's hair. Lost in my own thoughts about the fact that *I had a baby girl,* it takes me a while to realize the room is empty.

I pull back away from Kira, wiping the tears that I put on her face, each one of them tearing another piece of my heart out. "I'm so sorry," I whisper to her.

She smiles sadly up at me, then pulls my head down, kissing my lips gently. "DaR, my love, you have nothing to be sorry for. I'm not crying because of what you did. I'm crying because of what one person's infatuation and the bad decision did and how many lives it destroyed. Samora ruined her sister's future, shamed her parents, took the woman you loved, and your children. The saddest part of all of it is, in the end, she gained nothing but a few moments of pleasure that she paid for until her last breath. It's just so sad."

"Where did everyone go? They all have to be so disappointed in me."

"You were and are grieving, DaR. Your boys would never think badly of you. Neither do the girls. If you would have seen how fired up Brittany and Luna were, it's a good thing she is dead, because those two girls were ready to rip Samora apart. I'm sure they will have a few questions, but now the attention has been turned to SiN."

"I wish he would just give me a chance to explain."

"DaR, if the tables were turned, who would you believe? The woman who raised you, or the man he was taught to hate? Come on, let's go home and call it an early evening. My man needs a good night's sleep and some snuggles."

For a split second I think I see a dark mist floating in the darkened corner of the room. I blink my eye only for it to be gone. Had SiN been here listening all along?

I vy

Wow, what a horrible story! I look around the room at all the colorful strangers. A few are whispering among themselves. Others looked pissed off and I feel like I have intruded on something very personal here. I look up at AvX, shocked at the anger I see on his face. I have never seen this side of him. He too is looking around and I can tell all the others in here are overwhelming him with their emotions.

I reach over and take his hand in mine, and immediately he relaxes as he smiles sadly down at me. I nod towards the door and he stands up. No one says a word as we walk out of the room.

He pulls me close after a few steps and kisses me on the forehead. I don't pull away because I think he needs the comfort right now and being in his arms is becoming one of my favorite places. That thought worries me though because I'm scared to get attached and then he may leave me too.

"What are you thinking about down there?"

"Couple things actually. I felt for your dad back there. That entire story was just so sad. It really shows you what your decisions can do to the people around you. Now that we are here, what's next?"

"I had Brittany prepare a room for you next to mine, and I thought that maybe we could spend some time chilling out. I don't know about you, but I am in desperate need of some downtime."

I stop dead in my tracks in the middle of a long hallway. "So, you're not planning on leaving me here?"

He stops looking down at me. "No, what would make you think that?"

"I… I just assumed once we got here you would drop me off and go on with your life."

He runs his hands through his hair and this is the first time he has ever looked at me in anger. "At what point did I give you that impression, Ivy? Did I ever say you are a pain in my ass and I'm dropping you off the first chance I get? Because that's the vibe I'm getting from you right now. You have turned my whole world upside down, but I'm still standing in this hallway with your body tucked into mine."

I look away from him and down at the floor. "You never said you were going to leave me. I just assumed you would be glad to get rid of me."

He gently caresses my cheek. "My poor Ivy, you have such a low opinion of everyone, you only expect to be disappointed. Because you are so doubtful and untrusting, I feel like your mind is your worst enemy. I'm going to give it to you straight because I'm tired of walking on eggshells with you. I plan on heading to our rooms, taking an actual shower, then probably a quiet dinner out on one of the balconies. Next rising, I had planned on taking you to some of my favorite places and see if I could coax that smile of yours to appear a little easier.

"I then plan on spending every rising with you until we figure out what we want to do, or not to do, but either way, we will be together. In other words, unless you tell me to go away and you never want to see me again, I'm going to be right here. I'm drawn to you like I have never been another and I'm willing to wait until you're ready, but what I won't allow is you pushing me away."

I smile and, for the first time in a long time, my heart doesn't feel so heavy. The hall ends, opening up into a huge, airy space. The sound of someone running towards us has both of us turning around. I hear a happy squeal and the next thing I know; a little green kid is launching herself into AvX's arms.

"Unka AvX, you're home. I was so worried, but I knew Papaw would find you. It just took forever." She kisses his cheek and wraps her little arms around his neck, hugging him tightly. Her eyes land on mine. I am shocked at their beautiful pink color. "You missed my birthday."

"I know, Sweetie, and I was trying really hard to find you something special."

"I see you found her?"

"I did, Keida, this is Ivy, but you already knew that, didn't you?"

She looks shyly over at me. "I saw her pretty hair, but I didn't know her name until now. Ivy,…will you be staying with us?"

I look over to AvX. "We are still working on that, but for now, yes."

She pulls his face right up to hers and lays her forehead on his, smiling. I hear her whisper, "I told you that you would find your special girl. You're lucky you're my favorite, and that I'm going to be eight for a while longer because I'm still waiting for my present. I think you should ask Ivy to help you decide what it should be."

He smiles back at her. "Do you think girls think up better presents than boys?"

She shrugs and starts to wiggle for him to put her down. She walks up to me and I reach out, running my hand through her beautiful brown and pink hair. Her features are stunning, even as a child.

"I told SeeSee and Raven about Tarra so that when she comes to see you, they won't chase her."

She touches my arm and I immediately feel calmer. My insides seem to settle for the first time in forever. Her pink eyes twirl like there is water behind them. "To make this journey and not fall deeply in love simply because you are afraid to try would be a sad way to celebrate the sacrifices you have had to make. Open your heart and ignore your mind. Follow the lights to your own happiness."

She lets go of my arm and twirls around towards a young boy I just noticed standing right behind her. "Come on, Danny, Papaw needs some hugs."

I watch as she skips out of the room. "Who is she again?"

My niece: she is XuL's and Brit's daughter. SoL and I compete over the best Unka title. Until you came along, she was my top priority. I'm sorry I didn't take the time to introduce you to everyone back there, but I had to get out of that room.

"I could tell by the look on your face you were struggling. The boy, he is human. How did he get here?"

"I'll tell you his story over dinner. Come on, let's go get settled."

He takes my hand, leading me off towards a corridor to the left. The little girl's words flow through my head over and over as I question. *Do I still have a heart to give, or will the darkness of my past drag us both down in the end?*

AvX stops suddenly, and I realize I have been lost in my own thoughts this whole way. "This is you, and I'm right next door. Your clothes and other goodies should already be here. There is a door that connects our rooms, but the lock is on your side, so you don't have to worry about me sneaking in. I'll give you a few hours to yourself and then we will have dinner on the balcony. If that's ok? I don't really feel like socializing this evening. My senses could use a break and after all that with Dad, well, it's going to be noisy in my head."

"That's fine with me. Just knock on the door when you are ready."

I stand by the door, watching him as he walks a few steps away. I almost follow him, but I stop myself and instead walk into another massively exquisite area. "Damn," I whisper to myself. "These people must be loaded to be able to live like this."

SAGE popping up in front of me has me grabbing my mouth to keep from screaming out. My heart is immediately beating out of my chest. "We have got to quit meeting like this, SAGE. You are going to give me a heart attack."

"I apologize once again. You do seem to be easily startled. I will try to announce myself from now on. I don't like being the cause of your distress. I simply popped in to see if you needed anything, and to check if your room was satisfactory."

"From what I can tell, the room is nicer than what I lived in at home. I was just thinking these people must be loaded."

"Master DaR and all his sons are financially stable. Master DaR worked hard as a youngling to make sure his younglings would always be provided well for."

"Speaking of finances, I have been living off everyone's charity so far. How does one go about getting a job on an…alien planet? At some point, I will have to find a way to support myself."

She shakes her head. "Nonsense, we will discuss this again at a later date if it still concerns you, but I would put that out of your mind for now. I was given orders from the Commander for you to be marked. If you would step into the bathing chamber, we can get that done before you change for, last meal."

"Marked with what? Like a tag or something?"

"Have you not noticed the house mark on all the others? I would have thought AvX would have explained this to you by now."

"I have no idea what you are talking about, and you ain't marking me with no damn cow tag."

I turn, looking for the door that is supposed to connect my room to AvX's. I reach for the handle and when the door opens, I rush into the room, SAGE hovering right behind me. When I don't see him anywhere in the main area, I head down a small hall. I'm so mad I can't see straight, so I don't pay attention to the sound of water running until I walk right into a bathroom and a naked AvX steps out of the shower.

I don't know who is more shocked, him or me. I can't stop my eyes from scrolling down his entire frame. The man has zero fat on him, his skin glistens in the bathroom lighting. And as much as I know it's wrong, I can't keep my eyes above his waist. Hanging down against his leg is—*ohhh my*. I think I may have dreamed up this pleasure rod of his because that's exactly what it was designed for. It's slightly darker blue than his skin, well, now I understand the term *ribbed for her pleasure* better. The more I look at him, the harder and longer it's getting.

SAGE's voice makes me jerk and I spin around. "Oh, god, AvX, I'm sorry. I didn't mean to barge in on you like that." I'm trying to wipe the smile off my face as I know that image of that,… will be forever burned into my brain.

I can hear him laughing behind me. "Maybe I should have had the lock put on my side instead. You can turn around now. I'm decent."

I hold my hands against my burning cheeks, knowing that there is no way I can look him in the eye ever again. So I walk out of the room. "I'll give you a minute to get dressed. I'll just wait in the other room." SAGE hovers right next to me and I swear she has a smile on her face.

He comes out a few minutes later in a pair of shorts only and I swear I have to stop myself from drooling. There has to be a law against such beauty on a man. He grins at me, and I squirm in my seat as I know he can feel how attractive I find him.

"So where's the fire, as Kira would say?"

"SAGE, says I have to be marked?"

"And?"

"Don't you AND me dammit! I'm tired of people just assuming I should do something. I have no idea what the hell she is talking about or why I need to be branded like a piece of livestock."

He frowns. "There you go again, getting all defensive over nothing. I'm simply going to assume that Father instructed SAGE to give you one of these." He turns his wrist over, showing me a mark I barely noticed before. "This is the mark of the House of DaR. It's a privilege to have, and at one time, very few wore this mark. It does multiple things for you, but none of them mark you as being owned by someone. I'm sure Father brought it up to secure your place in society. This House mark provides safety, currency, and a sense of belonging. This is my family's mark and I would be honored for you to wear it openly for all to see."

"Ohhh, damn, I'm sorry. I jumped to conclusions. Will it hurt?"

SAGE speaks up. "Mistress Ivy, if you would follow me into your bathing chamber, we can get this done rather quickly, and no, it is not painful."

I stand up hesitantly, looking at each of them.

"Come on, I'll go with you."

AvX walks behind me, his hand on the small of my back. I follow SAGE's form, as I'm not sure where the bathroom is since I stormed out before I could look around.

SAGE hovers over what looks like a blood pressure sleeve. "Simply put your arm in this and I will let you know when to remove it."

I have to make myself put my arm in that thing. I know SAGE says it won't hurt, but how does she know? She is a damn projected image. The machine beeps and AvX pulls my arm out slowly. I rub my hand over the mark, staring down at the intricate details and amazed that my skin doesn't even feel hot.

"This won't rub off?"

"Nope, it's similar to what you would call a tattoo on Earth."

I reach over and take his arm, comparing the two marks. His arm lights up around my fingertips. "This mark is beautiful, but nothing compared to these." I run my hand up his arm, watching the scroll's light as they follow my fingertips. "Why do they do this?"

"You are not ready for that conversation, but I promise I will tell you one rising. Do you want to change, or would you like a snack?"

"I could handle a snack."

"SAGE. We will be on the outer balcony facing the dark forest. Could you send out some refreshments?"

CHAPTER 24

I^{vy}

A COOL BREEZE blows across the balcony we are sitting on. Strange birds fly through the trees, their sounds oddly soothing. I take a deep breath. My belly is full, I'm not hurting anywhere, and it's nice to stop for a minute and unwind. AvX is quiet this evening, but it's not uncomfortable.

I take the time to look around, amazed at the different colors surrounding us. I can't remember the last time I just sat down with absolutely nothing to do. Back home, life was crazy. I was either at work, having to do something for mom, or hanging out with friends. I don't know if this is relaxing or unsettling.

The wind picks up, blowing a few strands of my hair into my face and before I can push them away AvX leans over, tucking them behind my ear.

"My mother always said, *when your mind is unsettled, listen to the wind, and you will know the direction to go.*"

"Too bad it doesn't come with better directions, huh? Your world is different, AvX, scary and amazing all at the same time. I would love to just take off walking, but at the same time I want to hide in my room."

"Ivy, there are times I feel the same way, especially after an interrogation or when I'm in a vast crowd. The interrogations are self-inflicting torture for me because I have to focus so hard on one individual. It is never a pleasurable affair because they are not being questioned for nothing. They are always criminals or something worse, but it's easy for me to tell if they are lying or leaving out key things. When I get in a group, especially if all my brothers are together, it can become just noise in my head. I have a hard time concentrating or even having a conversation in a crowd sometimes. Now on Mother's planet, our kind has learned to cloak their emotions and not project them, so it's easier for me to mingle there. I'm sorry I have been quiet this darkness. This is the first peace I have had in ages; it seems."

"I don't mind you being quiet. It's nice to just be sometimes. When I was a kid, I spent a lot of time on the porch alone, reading or listening to music. With that thought, I'm sure I will have to learn your language now or I won't understand anything."

"Not particularly. SAGE has converted everything in our dwellings to your English. I will show you how to switch it over if it hasn't been reset. If you would like, I'll get you a personal holo pad. I believe Luna and Kira both use theirs to read their Earthly romances on, also ANDI has a huge backlog of the music from your planet. I will warn you ahead of time though, don't be shocked to find him or SAGE dancing to some of their favorite human songs."

"You mean, I can read books and listen to music from back home?"

"Absolutely."

"That's so freaking awesome! Damn,… I thought everything was gone."

"If I would have known it would make you this happy, I would have saved it as a surprise."

"I'm surprised, so you win either way."

"Too bad Keida isn't this easy. I have shopped over the cosmos only to come up empty-handed. I was so sure I would find the perfect present for her when I took off."

"Oh, girls are easy, you boys just overthink everything. We all like the same things. Pretties, whether it's jewelry or even a damn rock with sparkles on it. We like mementos, like pictures, or trinkets that have a meaning. What is she into?"

"Swords, and fighting."

"I'm sure she is doing that for a reason, but she is still all girl. You could tell that by the way she was dressed. Her hair was perfectly braided away from her face and her clothes were designed specifically to show off her features. When I was little, I had a locket that had my mom's picture in it. I never took it off. When I lost it, I was devastated."

"That's a wonderful idea, but she wouldn't be able to wear it if she was practicing. Wait a minute; SAGE, are you busy?"

"Ding, ding."

"What is that noise?"

"It's me, Master AvX. I told Mistress Ivy I would warn her before I popped in from now on. Can I be of service?"

I turn away, trying not to laugh. After all, she did exactly as I asked her to do. AvX looks at me and I shrug, acting completely innocent.

"Ok, I'm going to pretend that wasn't overly weird out of either of you. SAGE, Ivy came up with an idea for a gift for Keida, but I'm not sure if we can make it work. I would like to have a hologram locket designed for Keida that she can wear no matter what she is doing. Inside, I want it to flip images of all of us. Is there a way to make it part of her uniform, or possibly merge with something so it's not lost or taken from her if in a battle? This would give her a piece of home, no matter where she is."

"Excellent idea, Master AvX. I will contact SCOUT and see if he can put me in touch with a designer. Would you like anything specific engraved in it?"

"The house symbol will be appropriate, I think."

"Excellent, and thank you. I was contemplating breaking something so that I would have an excuse to contact SCOUT. Now I don't have to."

She pops back out and I can't help but laugh. "She is really stuck on this SCOUT guy, isn't she?"

"Oh, yeah, and I swear she gets bolder about it every day. It's so funny. I don't know about you, but I'm exhausted."

"I think you have every right to be tired." I stand up, straightening the cushions and picking up the plates our odd food had been on.

"Ivy, you don't have to do that. SAGE will clean all this up."

"How? She doesn't have arms."

"She has Worker bots to help out with what she calls everyday chores here at the main dwelling."

"I feel bad leaving this for someone or thing to clean up."

"You sound like Kira. She refuses to have them in her house because she says they don't do it to suit her and she is perfectly capable of cleaning up after herself."

"Kira, that's your dad's,… wife, girlfriend? I'm not sure what to call her."

"She is his mate. They are soul bound, which is very rare."

"She was stunning, hell all of them in that room were."

"Yes, I completely agree. They all are beautiful inside and out."

It takes me a second to realize he is including me in that statement and I can feel myself blush. I smile and shake my head as we head back down the hallway towards my room. We come to my closed door and I hesitate to walk through it. Before I can make a move myself AvX turns me towards him, leaning down to put his forehead on mine.

"I really enjoyed this evening."

"I did too."

He puts a finger under my chin, tilting my head up towards his. His lips brush across mine gently, and I wrap my arms around his neck. My body practically jolts as he pulls me in tightly. I groan as the taste of him hits my tongue. The connection between us blazes as brightly as those solar flares did in space. I have never felt this attraction with anyone else. I feel like a moth being lured into the light that seems to pulse all over his skin.

He pulls away first and I feel him reach behind me, opening the door. "You better go on before I can't stop. You are way more tempting than you know, my little human."

I pull my arms off his neck and head into the other room as he shuts the door behind me. My whole body buzzes as I try to push this extreme attraction I have for him away. I need to take a shower and go to bed before I turn around and tackle him.

"Ding, ding."

"SAGE. I appreciate you trying to make me more comfortable, but you don't have to warn me you're here. I get it."

"As you wish, I wanted you to know that the Ionizing shower is still something you haven't got to experience and all the other females love it if they're tired or in a hurry. I also have designed a couple of sleeping gowns a little more appropriate for your young age. I had ANDI send me some pictures of the clothing in your era and hope that they are to your liking."

"Thank you, SAGE; you have been so nice to me. I really appreciate you taking the time to make me feel more comfortable. Lord knows I feel like a fish out of water."

"You will adjust, as have all the others. Come, let me show you the Ionizer."

I take my clothes off and step into what feels like a phone booth. Dry air hits me, moving my hair up and off my shoulders. It tells me to move certain ways and then informs me that I can now exit. I step out and immediately raise my arm to smell my armpit.

Amazed that there is no odor at all. When I walk back over towards a mirror, my hair lay shiny in small waves. *'Now this is what I'm talking about'* I whisper.

SAGE pops up in the mirror. "The Ionizer will spoil you, especially if you are in a hurry, but I have learned you humans still like a long bath and a shower occasionally. Master DaR just had the showers installed in the family home. Anything his Kira likes; he makes sure is available anywhere she may need it. Your gowns are in the top drawer with the matching undies. If you need me through the night, don't hesitate to yell out. I will hear you."

I pull the gown out on top and slide it on. The material is so thin it's like wearing nothing at all, and if I turn a certain way, I'm not going to leave much to the imagination, with the high slits on the sides and the small spaghetti straps that are holding it just a couple inches above my boobs. The panties don't hide much more, but at least all the vital parts are covered. Walking out of the bathroom, I sort of wander around looking at everything. Several times I stop in front of our adjoining door, wondering what he is doing on the other side.

I finally make myself head back towards the vast bedroom and crawl under the covers. The bed is soft and the sheets feel great against my skin. I try to snuggle down, but all I keep doing is tossing and turning. The room is too quiet, and there are weird noises, shadows seem to be closing in on me. I keep telling myself it's just my imagination and the fact that this is the first night I have been alone since this hell all started for me. After what feels like forever, I sling the covers off and sneak up to that door again, sticking my ear against it to see if I can hear anything.

I open it slowly, sticking my head in before tiptoeing to his bedroom. The room is dark, but there is still enough light for me to see him sprawled across the side, laying on his belly, his breathing slow and steady. I lift one side of the covers up and slowly crawl in, trying not to jar him awake. He doesn't move at all as I turn on my side, facing him. I can feel his body heat seeping through the blankets, even though he is a few inches away from me. Yawning, it doesn't take long before sleep pulls me under.

CHAPTER 25

AvX

I HEAR her soft footsteps approaching the bed. Her emotions reach out, begging for comfort and familiarity. I decide to lay still to see what she is going to do. A cool draft drifts over my back as she lifts the covers and crawls in. Within minutes, her mind settles and she relaxes into sleep. I raise up, turning my head towards her now sleeping form.

Slowly, I turn all the way towards her, amazed at how young and peaceful she looks sleeping. A piece of her long hair lay in soft waves across her shoulder. I pick it up, rubbing it gently between my fingers as my eyes roam over her. Her skin is now flawless and pale beside a few dark spots across one cheek. This is the first time I have been able to enjoy her at leisure. We have been thrown together in a whirlwind of nonstop events and it is nice to be able to stop and gaze at her beauty.

I pull her over to me and tuck her head into my chest, my chin resting on top of hers. Ivy fits against me like a missing piece of puzzle I have been searching for my whole life. She sighs, snuggling in closer, and I simply let myself enjoy the moment. I'll worry about the next rising when it comes.

Opening my eyes, it seems like I no sooner closed them that the suns are coming back up. I'm relieved that this last darkness was not a dream, as I can still feel her body curled up next to mine. My hand is wrapped around a long, naked leg that is draped casually over my hips. We must have shifted around in the bed last darkness as Ivy is now tucked into my side, her head laying on my chest. Looking around, I take the time to simply enjoy the peacefulness, as I know the moment she awakens in my arms, all of this will change. For a second, I almost untangle myself from her and get up, but she feels so good against me, I can't make myself move. She starts squirming around and the second she opens her eyes. I sigh as I look down at her, awaiting her ire of waking up in my arms.

"Did you come in here to seduce me, my little human? You are tempting me greatly and if you don't stop moving that leg, I might have to teach you a lesson on what happens to little females who sneak into a male's bed."

Instead of jerking out of my arms like I thought she would, she lays her head back down on my chest, not saying a word. Her small fingers trace the indentions on my chest as my runes flare brightly with her touch.

"Why do they do this? I have asked you this several times, but you always change the subject."

"I'm not sure you are ready for that answer."

"Is it bad?"

"Depends. I never know how you are going to react."

"If it makes you feel any better, I never know how I'm going to either. You don't seem to be upset by finding me in your bed."

"This is the best rising I can ever recall. The fact that you are allowing me to hold you like this means the world to me."

"I couldn't sleep, the room—the everything—was, and is, just too wrong. You are the only place that seems normal. How screwed up does that sound?"

"You don't hear me complaining."

"Honestly, I don't think I have heard you complain or bitch about anything. I have done enough of that for both of us."

Her hand starts moving lower and my shaft jumps. "Ivy, you're in dangerous territory."

She rubs her nose against my skin. "You smell so good, and the texture of your skin feels amazing next to mine." She takes a deep breath and I can tell she is worried about telling me something. "I don't want to sleep anywhere else, AvX, and I don't want a room of my own. I want to be with you, wherever that is. You act like you care about me and lord knows I wouldn't be here without you, but I don't want you to feel obligated because I was forced upon you. If you don't want more, I understand and I'll go if you want me to. Am I pushing you too hard, or are we moving too fast?"

"When you know, you know in my world, Ivy. I understand in your culture humans in general don't have a way to recognize their soul mates. However, that's not the case with many other species. My runes lit up fully for the first time, the moment I put you in my arms. Every time you touch me, they reach for you. The light of my soul is trying to link ours together. I have stood in a room full of emotions and family and felt completely alone until I had you beside me. I have waited and searched for something all my life, never knowing what it was until… you. I promise I will never stray, leave, or harm you in any way. My only goal in this life now is to take those shadows out of your eyes and replace them with the sparkle of happiness. I'm not going anywhere, Ivy. You can feel free to force yourself on me at any time, and if friendship or someone to hold you in darkness is all you ever want from me, that is fine, too. Even your harsh words and doubts will not push me away. I will stand by you until the Lord of Light takes my last breath."

She pushes up and one of the small straps falls off her shoulder, the top of her breast bared to me, and I have to make myself look away. "You're not going to leave me, even for a cute Smurfette?"

"No."

"You don't feel responsible for me?"

"Yes, but not in the way you're thinking. I don't believe I could handle another male stepping in to take you from me. You are mine, Ivy, to provide and take care of, whether you want me or not."

She pulls the blankets down off me, tracing my runes as they chase after her fingers. She hesitates at the seam of the shorts I have on, even though there is no missing how hard my shaft is under them. I groan when she brushes her hand along its length over the material.

"Ivy, I only have so much control, and having your half-naked body pressed up against mine all darkness already has me pushed to my limits, don't tease me unless you are willing to pay the consequences." I have to fist my hands together to keep from grabbing her as she explores my chest.

She leans forward, her feelings towards me no longer jumbled, but now more determined. Her mischievous smile is all the warning I get before she slides her hand under my shorts, grabbing my shaft firmly in her small hand. I arch off the bed, seizing her body, stretching her across my chest as I bring her mouth to mine.

"You were warned."

"I have never been good at following the rules," she whispers back to me.

I grasp the back of her head and pull her lips to mine, devouring her like a male starved. Her hand never stops working my shaft as I plumage her mouth. All coherent thoughts leave my head as her hand pumps me up and down. My own slickness now coating her hand as my body craves release.

"You are so fracking soft. How did I ever come to deserve you?" Half sitting up, I take a claw, cutting through the flimsy little straps holding her gown up. It slides down, pooling around her hips.

She makes a small sound of surprise and I can feel her pleasure as I snag her pink nipple into my mouth. Her hand leaves my shaft as she pulls me close with both arms.

"I will never get enough of these, you. I plan on tasting all of you, my little human. I believe this luscious body of yours has pushed me to the point of no return. If you want me to stop, you better tell me now."

My tongue meanders down her chest while my hands explore her body. Every moan and gasp pushing me on. Twisting our bodies, I pull her under me. She peers up at me, desire sparkling through her eyes as she gazes up. I slowly lower myself down her body, pulling what remains of her gown with me as I gradually unwrap her. I can feel her trust and her acceptance push through my mind. The fact that she wants me as much as I want her makes me feel like I'm floating in the clouds.

I slide my hands down her long legs, pulling them up and over my shoulder as I open her up wide in front of me. The smell of her arousal has me to the point of embarrassing myself. Her inner thighs are slick with her own juices as her body aches to be filled with mine.

Lowering my head, I rub my nose through her tender folds. Then I lick her sweet flesh, teasing her as she gasps and cries out. I run my tongue from the bottom to the top of her slit, absorbing her essence into myself. Then my tongue lands on a hardened nub of her pretty pink slit, and she jerks when I lick it. I can feel what her body is screaming out for, and this is the magical button that will make her mine.

"Frack, Ivy, you taste so good. I am barely holding on here." She arches off the bed, grabbing my hair as she grinds against my face, trying to pull me closer. Without missing a beat, I slide one finger inside of her tight channel. She groans out as her body starts to shake and tremble. I can feel that she is close.

Pressing a second finger into her, my hand pounds faster as I suck on this hardened nub that is bringing her so much pleasure. This is the first time I have ever been this in tune with another's needs. Her hold on my hair tightens and the sound that leaves her throat as her body convulses around my hand is one of long-denied pleasure.

I lick and suck until her body calms and she tries to push me away from her sensitive channel. I yank the shorts I had on off, having to feel her skin against mine.

"Tell me to stop, Ivy, because if I take you now, there will be no escaping me. I will chase you to the corners of the universe. Do you understand me?"

"Make me yours, AvX."

I grab my shaft, rubbing it through her slick folds. She wraps her long legs around me, pulling me forward as I gradually enter into her. "Ivy love, relax." Her body fights my entrance, making each of my gentle thrust torture. I reach down, tugging her up, kissing her swollen lips as her body finally accepts all of me.

I thrust in and out slowly at first, giving her small channel time to get used to my size. She feels so delicate and small in my arms as I surge forward gently.

"AvX, stop holding back and give me what both of us want. You feel so good. I never knew it could be like this."

Her words push my conscious thought away as I thrust into her. Her small nails claw at my skin as our bodies come together. I manage to hold back long enough to feel her shatter once again, her pleasure milking my shaft as I yell out my own release. Collapsing onto my side, I pull her close, our bodies slick and damp laying here entangled together. Our hearts beat frantically as our minds process the intenseness of our mating. I pull the covers back over us when I feel her shiver next to me. "Did I hurt you?"

"If that's pain, sign me up."

She glances up at me with a smile on her face, only to sit up abruptly. Her breast dangling close to my face has me reaching out, grabbing one sucking it into my mouth. She pulls away, a worried look on her face. "AvX, what is this? You have a new mark on your face and it's moving down your neck."

I shrug. She starts scrambling out of the bed. "Come on, you need to see this."

I let her pull me out of the bed only so I can watch her ass shake as she walks in front of me. I smack her playfully on the butt as we walk through the refresher's door.

"Look." She points towards the viewing wall. I walk up to the viewer and move my head back and forth. I know what the mark is the moment I see it. All Valerian males wear the mark of their mates on their faces for all to see. What I didn't expect to see is matching ones now forming on Ivy's skin.

I pull her in front of me, my shaft enjoying the feel of her skin as I press myself into her. I put my hands over her eyes before she looks into the viewer at herself. She had been so preoccupied with me she never took the time to look in the viewer. She wiggles against me and I place my hand on her stomach, loving how the color of my skin contrasts so much with hers in the viewer. "Now don't freak out on me."

I take my hands away and she looks up at me, worried. I point towards the viewer and her eyes immediately get large. Her small hand comes up to her cheek where glowing blue marks now mark her beautiful skin.

"They're the same?"

"Yes, the one on your cheek is the soul mark of my kind. I never thought to warn you because I have not ever seen another species wear the Valerian mark. I'm sorry, I should have said something. Are you angry?"

She doesn't answer me at first, just turns to the viewer, watching more of my markings form all over her right side. The swirls and designs curve around her hip and stomach, then spreads out over her shoulder and neck before ending at her cheek.

"This is permanent, everyone and anyone who sees them knows that I'm yours?"

"Correct." My heart is beating out of my chest right now and I can't figure out what she is feeling. That's odd, I can't seem to read her like I always have been able to.

She turns, practically bouncing into my arms, wrapping her long legs around me while I squeeze her soft butt cheeks.

"Does these symbols mean you love me?"

"Love is not a big enough word to emphasize the feelings I have for you, my little human, but yes, I love you. With or without my marks upon your beautiful skin."

"What an adventure we've had, huh? I never dreamed or even hoped to be loved, but now that I have you, I can't imagine a day without you in it. I…love you too, AvX."

CHAPTER 26

A^{vX}

I smack her bare bottom before lowering her down. "As immeasurably as I would love to stay in bed with you all rising, I have been dying to show you something. Go get dressed, I think, as much as you enjoyed the shuttle trip yesterday you will love the new hovercraft SCOUT has invented. Meet me back here in ten."

"What do I need to wear?"

"SAGE."

"Yes, Master AvX?"

"Does Ivy have suitable swimming attire?"

"No, but I can have several ready for her momentarily."

"We are going swimming?"

"Sorta; go on before I can't keep my hands off you."

She runs out of the room, her laughter echoing off the walls, and for the first time in my life, I feel complete. I step into the Ionizer and then dress, taking my time as I expect she may be awhile.

"I'm ready, are you?" I hear her yell out.

"Coming." I whistle as I walk into the main living quarters. "Look at you, I swear you get more beautiful every rising, and sorry, I figured you would be a little bit."

I grab her hand and as we approach a side wall; it disappears and we walk into what XuL calls a garage.

"I'm never going to get used to the disappearing wall thing." Her emotions seem more settled, and her excitement is being projected loudly.

I pull one of the hover sleds out and activate its features before laying it on the floor. "Ok, just step on."

We both step up at once and the board tilts for a second. Ivy grabs onto me, laughing. I pull her close and the board lifts off the ground effortlessly now that it has calibrated our combined weight. "Hold on."

SAGE had already input the coordinates, so all I had to do was hold Ivy and enjoy the ride. We leave the main part of the dwelling and the board hovers about five feet above the ground as it rushes us through the grass fields and off to our destination.

"Wooohooo!" Ivy yells out as we float quickly across the ground. "This is awesome." Her laughter fills my soul.

A small lake and waterfall come into sight within a few minutes and she reacts just the way I hoped. "Oh my, would you look at that?"

The hover sled lowers all the way to the ground and I pick her up, carrying her the rest of the way to a natural sandy beach.

"I can walk, you know."

"Humor me, I like having you in my arms."

"Good thing it's one of my favorite places to be."

A blanket and a basket full of snacks has already been provided for us, thanks to SAGE. She also activated the Guard bots, so the only worry I have the rest of the rising is enjoying Ivy.

She walks over after flipping her sandals off, sticking her toes into the water lapping at the bank as she pulls the cover she has on over her clothes off. "It's warm?"

The sight of her standing in front of that waterfall in those two small strips of material with my marks shimmering in the suns will forever be burned into my head. Her long hair flows around her body wildly as the wind off the waterfall mists our way.

"Do you know how to swim?"

"Hey, Earth girls do come with a few skills, but is there anything in there going to try to eat me?"

I run towards her, grabbing her around the waist as I launch us into the air, turning in time so that her body doesn't smack the water. Her startled scream ends just as the water swallows us. I kick my legs hard, bringing us right back up to the surface.

Ivy's huge smile greets me as we clear the water. I brush her long hair back off her face as she splashes me playfully. She wraps her legs around my waist and drapes her arms around my neck. One of the strips of her bathing attire slips down, her nipple barely holding the material up.

"You butt munch, you could have warned me."

"What fun is that?"

She pulls me close, kissing me playfully, before I unwrap her legs and throw her up into the air. Her laughter is addictive as I catch myself smiling so wide my jaws are hurting. She pops back up, her top now unraveled and floating in the water. I duck under the water, swimming around her long legs, coming up behind her. Pulling her cool skin back against mine, I grasp her breast in both hands.

"I think you have been lying to me this whole time about being a human. You are actually a water temptress out to seduce any male who comes within your reach."

She entwines her legs with mine as she wiggles her butt against me. I kiss the water off her neck, tracing the symbols that mark her as mine. Turning her in my arms, I slowly work her bottoms off so that I can enjoy her naked body fully.

"I think you have way too many clothes on, mister."

She raises a leg up, hooking one of her toes inside my waistband and drags my shorts off my shaft already seeking her out as it nudges her sensitive folds. She wraps her long legs around my waist as I effortlessly keep us afloat.

My hands wander down her curvy frame, one settling on her pleasure button as she arches in my arms, grinding against my hand, her body screaming out for more. I line my shaft up, rubbing it back and forth on her slit, making sure her body is ready for mine, and with one thrust, I'm seated fully. Ivy lets out a long moan as her body clamps down on mine. I almost forget we're in the water and we start to sink.

Ivy pulls me close, sucking on my earlobe and kissing my neck while my hands grasp her hips tightly as I thrust into her forcefully enough that we are making waves in the water. I feel her body start to tremble and I know she is close. I make myself hold off until I feel her inner folds grasp my shaft tightly. Our moans echo throughout the valley as my own release makes my legs weak and we start to sink into the water.

I push off the bottom and the moment we break the surface, Ivy's smile and laughter lighten my soul. "We so have to do that again."

We spend the rest of the rising, either making love, playing in the water, or laying on the beach snacking as the suns warmed our skin. Ivy's smiles and laughter make her appear whole, unlike the creature I got out of that cage, and I have never felt more complete.

SAGE delivers a change of clothing as darkness approaches, and reluctantly, I let Ivy get dressed. Her body is covered in little love bites, and her lips are swollen from my kisses. She seems to be glowing. No one would ever know by looking at her now the horrors she has gone through.

"I hate for this day to end."

"Oh, we will have many more days like this one. I have an entire universe to show you. Before we head back this darkness, I figured you would want to check on Tarra."

"Is she close?"

"I can't believe she isn't already here. Your screams of ecstasy could be heard throughout the galaxy."

She blushes. "I am not the only screamer, mister."

Ivy gathers a few of her things and I send out a prayer to the Lord of Light for bringing us together. I will spend eternity proving I'm worthy of the gift he has bestowed upon me.

This time we manage to hop right onto the hover sled, and it takes right off flying alongside the dark forest as we approach

Tarra's new nest site. I hear her calling out to us before we ever get close.

"Pretty girl, where are you?" Ivy yells out.

I turn the hover when I see a flash of light coming out of one of the Guardians. "Look up there." I point up into one of the massive guardian trees.

Slowly, I start increasing our height until we are only feet below Tarra. She looks out from her massive nest, but she doesn't fly down to see us like I thought she would. She projects protection, and that puzzles me.

She lets out an odd squawk, and the Guardian lowers her massive limb down to our height, as the hover will go no higher.

Ivy grabs my arm. "AvX, jump, the tree is falling."

I can't help but laugh when she says this. "Ivy, I would like to introduce you to Guardian Elowen. She has taken over as a protector for Tarra and her young."

"Her young, and who is Elowen? I only see Tarra?"

"Elowen is the name of the Guardian tree she has built her nest in. I'll explain it more to you later. Look." Tarra flares out her wings, showing off the three small eggs she is sitting on. I have to grab Ivy as she starts to bounce up and down.

"Tarra, you're gonna be a momma. Oh my god, I'm so excited. We will come visit every day. Pretty girl, I can't wait to see your babies."

All at once the large male AllTarra swoops down out of the sky, settling himself behind Tarra, cooing as he rubs his head against her.

"You better be good to my girl, or we will have you for dinner, birdbrain."

The male looks up at Ivy, squawks once again, then simply ignores us like we're not there. Tarra reaches a long wing out, caressing Ivy's face before turning towards her mate. The Guardian raises her limb back and away from us as I start lowering the hover sled back to the ground and we head back towards the main dwelling. I hope that the gift that SAGE is preparing for Keida is ready for both of my girls.

CHAPTER 27

A vX

WE GET BACK to the main dwelling, both of us still giggling like two younglings as we enter into my main chamber.

"Master AvX, Mistress Ivy. Kira has requested you two for a late supper. It will be a small affair. She is excited to meet the newest addition to our family."

"No problem SAGE, we will be along as soon as we get dressed. Oh, and SAGE, I need you to move Ivy's things into my main apartments."

"I already anticipated this move and her belongings have already been moved and put away."

"Thank you, SAGE."

"My pleasure, as always."

"She is quite handy to have around, isn't she?"

"Absolutely, to the point she spoils us and I catch myself calling out for her when I'm away from here. My mother thought it was hilarious the first time I did it in her company."

"You seem close to your mom."

"She is the first female I ever loved. I honestly can't believe she hasn't called already on the holo comm. Usually, it's an every-rising thing. It's probably the solar storms. She will be very excited to meet you."

"You don't think she will be upset I'm not… one of you?"

"Knowing my mother, she saw you coming and refused to tell me. I promise she will try to steal you away from me."

"Maybe you should see if you can get through to her. I wish I could call mine."

"We will do it together after a late dinner. Come now, no sad thoughts. Go get dressed and wear whatever you want. There is no hurry."

I have just sat down and pulled out my personal holo to see how many messages I've missed when she walks back into the room. Once again, she surprises me with how quickly she gets ready.

"Frack, you are beautiful. Maybe we will just stay here instead. I don't know if I will be able to handle the thoughts going around the room about how tempting you are."

"Quit it, it's just a sundress. Come on, let's go before I chicken out and allow you to keep me here permanently."

We walk into the dining area off the atrium, which I had to drag Ivy out of because she was overwhelmed by the fact this is in someone's home. Multiple voices and emotions hit me at once and I wince.

Ivy grabs my arm, looking up at me, and the noise seems to quiet down. I don't have time to think about it before Kira is walking our way with her arms out. One thing all us males love about Kira is her hugs. She always makes us feel welcome.

"AvX, darling, you have been hiding, haven't ya? I ran everyone off but a few; I hope that makes it easier for you. And who is this little beauty?"

"Kira, this is Ivy."

"Oh, sweet thing, come here and give me a hug."

I see Ivy tear up when Kira grabs her close. Kira pulls back and wipes a random tear off Ivy's cheek. "Now, none of that. There will be plenty of time for tears later."

"I'm sorry, you just caught me off guard. If I had closed my eyes, I would have sworn it was my mother talking."

"I'll never replace her, but I promise I will protect you like you are my own, so maybe that makes me a second momma to all these brats."

Ivy's emotions are quiet, and I know she is slightly upset. The room is loud in my head and it makes me stop her before we get any closer. I reach out, grabbing her hand in mine. "You ok?"

"Her voice shocked me, but I'm fine, really. I know I'm going to have ups and downs, but as long as I have you, I'll fight my way through it. Don't get me wrong, there are moments I'm forcing a smile, just because I don't want to dwell on the things that have happened, but I can't change five seconds ago, so I might as well try to make the minutes to come worth all the pain and loss."

I pull her close, kissing her cheek, but when I let go of her hand the room gets loud again. This time it's very noticeable and if it hadn't been for Keida tugging on my shoulder, I would have questioned it more.

I reach down, picking her up, observing how long her legs are getting. "Have you grown a foot in two days?" I grab one leg, shaking it playfully. "Where did all these come from? Here, I'll put you down and you can hold me."

"Unka AvX, stop it, you too big."

"Not at the rate you're growing. Before long, I won't be able to pick you up and that makes me sad, but I have something for you. Ivy, can you come here a moment?"

Ivy turns towards me and smiles up at Keida. Now that I have my two best girls here with me, I want to give you guys something. I reach into the side pocket on my vest and pull out a pale pink bag first. I hand it to Keida. "Open it."

With a big grin on her face, she opens the small pouch and pulls out the locket I had made for her.

"Oh, it's so pretty. Thank you, Unka AvX."

"Wait, that's not the surprise. Open it up."

She opens the locket gently. The second the clasp is released; small pictures start flipping through the frames on each side. "Look, there is you, now Mommy, and Papaw. Unka AvX, you're the best I told ya you would get me the best thing ever if you just asked Ivy."

"So, you like it?"

"I love it." She wraps her little arms around my neck and hugs me tight. "Would you put it on me, Ivy?"

"I would be happy to. AvX, turn her around a little so I don't get this wrapped up in her long hair."

I hold her away from me. Keida's emotions are so full of happiness and love I could hold her forever. Then Ivy touches my arm and everything goes quiet. Keida just smiles at me.

"You felt it, didn't you, Unka AvX?" she whispers in my ear.

"I felt something, little one, but I'm confused. Are you doing that?"

"Nope, that's all Ivy. You see, she is special, and I knew when you found her, she would be the one who finally gave you the peace you seek."

Ivy finishes clasping the necklace. "There you go. It looks so pretty against your skin."

Keida holds out her hand, and Ivy takes it in hers. "Ivy, I want you to think of something really loud."

I laugh because she projects that she is hungry.

"Now, make your mind quiet."

I see Ivy's expression change, but I can't feel anything from her at all.

"Keida, I'm enjoying our game here, but what's going on?"

"She is your shield. Ivy can block the noise that invades your mind all the time. All she has to do is touch you. She can also guard her own thoughts against you in the same way. You two are soul bound. Her marks are more than just pretty blue scrolls upon her skin."

Ivy looks up at me, her eyes wide, a small smile on her face tells me she is happy with this news. Kira yells out it's time to eat and Keida wiggles out of my arms. "Hey, before you take off, you won't have to worry about taking your locket off when you're practicing. Touch the center moon in the middle of the house symbol and it will merge with your skin."

"You are the best, Unka AvX." She darts off and I have to envy all her energy.

"Do you think what she said was true?"

"We will play with it some later. Let's go enjoy dinner."

I hold out a chair for Ivy and settle down beside her. Father, Kira, Grandfather, Victoria, XuL, and Britt are the only ones here this darkness, but it's still noisy.

Grandfather bends over the table looking at me. "I see that you are back in the number one spot of favorite Unka again, AvX?"

"I earned that one this time. If you all didn't know already, this is my Ivy."

Hellos and welcomes echo around the table as we all start filling up our plates. Dinner goes rather quickly and I try to force all the noise away so I can enjoy being here. Ivy must have realized I was struggling. She reaches over, taking my hand in hers, and immediately the room silences. Their actual voices are all I hear. I take a deep breath and whisper, "Thank you."

The girls all get up and Kira comes around, making sure Ivy is not left out. "Come on dear, let the guys go do manly stuff while we go talk about something more interesting... like them." Her laughter has everyone smiling.

I watch Ivy walk away, happy to see she appears to be fitting in well. It seems like she has stopped fighting everything and has opened her heart up to the changes that were forced upon her.

Father's voice has me turning back towards them. "AvX, son, I may have need of your special talents in a few rotations."

We walk off as he continues to tell me about the pirates EvO is in pursuit of. I listen halfheartedly, as all I want to do is grab Ivy and hide in our room for a few rotations.

Grandfather's laughter brings me back. "DaR, I believe you lost him a while back. His mind is with his mate." He pats me on the back. "Being away from her will get easier with time, but I believe me and your father both will agree, the pull never fades. Come, let's join the females. I'm positive they are having more fun than we are."

The girls all seem to be in a very in-depth conversation. Kira is the first one to say anything when we walk in.

"DaR, TY… you have to hear this story of Ivy's. Go ahead, dear, tell them what you told us."

"I was saying that the first time I saw AvX, I thought he was an Egyptian god. When I was in school, their culture fascinated me and I read everything I could find about their long-lost cultures and the gods they believed in. There were several pharaohs whose skin was reported to be blue, and they wore masks to cover their other world features. In their earliest reins, one of their pharaohs, Thutmose, wrote of a man falling from the sky in a tubular craft. This male later on took over. They called him Alulim, or maybe it was Anubis. I don't remember exactly, but he ruled for years and was the reason their culture was so advanced."

Victoria gets up, walking around the room. "TY, do you think it could have been Allaric? We never ventured into that part of the world. He could have landed there easily."

"Vic, I looked into Egypt some years later when I came across some of their writings, but I didn't investigate it thoroughly because the figure just disappeared."

Ivy speaks up, "He probably just went underground with the other pharaohs in death valley. They say the underground tunnels there are amazing and you could easily get lost in them. They have found chambers that resemble homes even."

Grandfather runs a hand through his hair and I can feel he is troubled by the conversation. "To think all that time, he may have been alive and by the time air travel was available, he had to hide, not knowing if any of us lived or died on the shuttle. Allaric wouldn't have been able to glamor himself because he wasn't from Darverius. He was a Valerian; their kind wasn't dependent on the Blood Beet like ours were. I will have ANDI pull up what remains. I'm sure his remaining family would like any information we could provide them."

I see Ivy yawn. "It's getting late. I think me and Ivy will turn in." I reach down, helping her out of her seat, and the room immediately quiets down in my head. Kira and Brittany both hug her before we leave and I can tell their kindness was much needed. We walk back towards our room. "Did you enjoy yourself?"

"Shockingly, I did, yes. I'm ready for a nice shower and some snuggle time."

"Sounds great to me." I pull her to a stop before we get to the door and take another pouch out of my pocket, this one blue, and hand it to her. "I was going to give this to you earlier, but we were interrupted."

She takes it out of my hand and looks at it oddly before opening it up. A gasp leaves her lips when she sees it. She holds the locket up by its chain, its reflection sparkling in the lights above us.

"My locket. How,… did you know? It looks exactly just like the one I lost years ago."

"ANDI helped me. I could tell how much it meant to you when you were talking about me making one for Keida, so I had ANDI do some research and he found a picture of you wearing it. SAGE then took the design and incorporated all the pictures they could find from Earth of you and your mother and, of course, there are a few of me in there so you won't forget me. The good thing is you can add to it anytime you want."

I take it out of her hand and she turns, lifting her hair out of the way so I can put it on. I hook the clasp and then kiss the back of her neck. Turning back towards me, she opens it slowly. The first picture is of her and her mother when she was little. We stand there for a few minutes as the pictures change before she shuts it back.

Wrapping her arms around my neck, she says, "You know this was very Smurfy of you. I think it's the best present I have ever received."

"Not me. It was the day I got you. I love you more than words can say,… my little human."

"And I love you, my alien Smurf."

THE END

OTHER BOOKS FROM THIS AUTHOR:

The Water Skippers series

Water Skippers

(Kyle and Eden)

A Dragonfly's Whisper

(Nora and Roman)

Earth Shadow

(Lorene and Garret) part one

Shadow Reborn

(Garret and Lorene)

Petal

(Randy and Petal)

Miranda and the Dragonfly King

(Miranda and Tagon)

Stand-alone novel

OTHER BOOKS FROM THIS AUTHOR:

The Playboy and the Waitress

The Forsaken series
Forsaken
(Lucas and Emma)
Betrayed
(Tavish and Eve)
Forgotten
(Tyberius and Victoria)
Spin off to DaR

Darverius
DaR
(DaR and Kira)
XuL
(XuL and Brittany)
SoL
(SoL and Alana)
RaZ
(RaZ and Katherine)
A House of DaR Celebration (novella)
Tordan
(Tordan and Luna)
Hugo
(Hugo and Miya)
AvX
(AvX and Ivy)

JENNIFER JULIE MILLER
WATER SKIPPERS SERIES
THE FORGOTTEN SERIES
HOUSE OF DaR SERIES
THE PLAYBOY

NOTE FROM THE AUTHOR

I hope... I have made you laugh, and possibly... even squeezed a few tears out of ya. Writing has been a lifelong dream for me, and our dreams are the only thing we have to build on!!!

So GO for it!!!!

I'm an avid reader myself. I believe there are Dragons, Unicorns, and multicolored Kitty Cats, because our imaginations are our own uniqueness.

I want to thank my family and friends for all your support.

To my readers, thank you for encouraging me to continue writing even though my worlds are a little different.

After all, I'm Appalachian, and I talk Appalachian. Therefore, I write Appalachian. All my books have country girls in them, and that's mainly because I only know how to speak country girl correctly.

Then to the Lord above, whose blessing gave a poor little girl from Ironton a chance to dream!

If you enjoyed this story, or any of my other ones, I ask that you take a few minutes of your time, and leave a review on Amazon, or Goodreads. It really helps new and older authors alike.

If you would like to stay in touch, hear about new releases, give some advice, or just drop a line.

You can find me on Facebook.

Https://facebook.com/JenniferJulieMiller.

On Twitter.

Https://www.twitter.com/jenniferrick

Or email me at:

Jenniferjuliemiller@gmail.com

Follow me on Bookbub. **Https://www.bookbub.com/pro-file/jennifer-julie-miller**

Follow me on Amazon.

Https://amazon.com/author/jjm5325903

And sign up for my email if you want to learn more about Darverius and DaR's twenty-two plus sons.

Http://eepurl.com/cfrL8X

FORSAKEN

Lucas and Emma

Katherine's parents

The one question she often asks herself is *why*. Why has she never been enough? Why doesn't anyone truly want her? She was reminded daily that she was nothing but a worthless girl and only another mouth to feed. The last time she saw her family was the night they dumped her in a ditch on the side of the road and left her to die.

A kind woman took her out of that ditch and gave her a home. Her new family was every girl's dream until a single poisoned scratch took it all away. Emma was tossed away again, becoming a prisoner and a slave to her circumstances. The one person the Cook enjoyed beating regularly. The day Cook sold her body, all of her hopes and dreams were destroyed. But one fateful night, after fighting for her life, she escapes this, Hell.

He finds her on the brink of death, naked, beaten, and barely alive. She thinks he is the Angel of Death, someone who will save her, but he is a real monster. Did she just trade one Hell for another? Will the memories he steals from her dreams soften his heart enough to make him care for something more than himself? Or will he turn her away, just to *Forsake* her, like all the rest?

BETRAYED

Tavish and Eve

It seems the ones we love the most are the first to Betray us! One such Betrayal cost me everything: my home, my dreams, and almost my life. The second I started running, I knew I would never be who I was or may have wanted to be. All of my choices were taken away with two last breaths, hers and then my own.

The dreams of my youth were destroyed because of the selfishness of others. I fear my life will become nothing but a cold existence of shadows and detachment.

The poison consuming my very soul is nothing but an excuse for me to lash out at the unfairness of it all. It's exactly the justification I need to deliver the pain others have inflicted on me my entire life. Will the emotions of my untried youth destroy my future as I'm forced into a world I truly don't understand?

My own mind has become my worst enemy, and my fragile heart can't withstand another break. I know he's a deceiver, a devil in disguise, sent to collect my grieving soul. He is the real monster my mother warned me about under the bed. If I let him, he will destroy me in the end with his mischievous smile and lying angel eyes.

To be loved is the only dream I have left, but we all know Betrayal is the one thing you can always count on to crush you.

FORGOTTEN

Tyberius and Victoria

(DaR's father)

I have known this evil was coming for me my whole life, but that doesn't mean I have looked forward to it! I have run from every sign of the darkness, even to the point of being invisible to the ones around me. I've spent my whole life lurking in the shadows of my family. Keeping myself separate from the ones I love, living my dreams, and wants through their eyes.

I had become so wrapped up in their worlds trying to ensure their happiness that the day he appeared in front of me. I never once questioned what I was supposed to do. The one thing my family could always count on is that I'm loyal to fault. Even though I made sure never to get too attached because I was terrified the darkness would take them also, it will do anything it can to defeat me. My goal is to survive and to finally see the light.

I have prayed to every God, for this to pass me by, only to know they can't answer. This is my destiny. I will suffer agony unlike anything my mind can imagine, but to be worthy of the light. I need to find a way to face this darkness.

I will never show him an ounce of weakness, but I scream silently for help. I refuse to let him win because he wants me here for eternity. A soul withered in ice, and loneliness, Forgotten in this room of horrors.

All the stars line up for us one time or another. I just have to wait my turn.

DAR

Kira

In the blink of an eye, my whole world has collapsed around me. Headed towards my dream vacation, I was snatched right out of the air. My husband, the love of my life, was destroyed right in front of my eyes. He fought bravely, trying to protect me from a horror neither one of us could have ever imagined. I find myself standing in the spotlight on a stage. Mutilated and tortured, the blood from my body flowing freely down my legs along with my will to live. Piercing yellow eyes emerge from the darkness, but even the shadows can't hide his imposing form. Gentle, but terrifying arms reach out for me and within their embrace, can I find the will to live again?

DaR

I am a bad ass, known throughout the galaxy for my brutality as a ruthless and feared commander. With that being said, somehow, I still got coerced into purchasing a slave. My eyes fall upon a small female whose very essence and eternal light is leaking out of her onto the floor below her. I watch in awe as she accepts her fate, willing her nightmare to be over. I almost turn away from her and the unnecessary cruelly in this room, but the very thought of her dying on that floor surrounded by the very monsters that have done this to her disgusts me. I walk up among the beings surrounding her and pull her from the stage, daring, or should I say, hoping, they try to do something about it. The moment I put her in my arms, everything changed. The attachments I have avoided my whole life become unavoidable. Will this damaged slave be able to replace the shadows in my life? One thing for sure is that I will destroy the entire universe to keep her safe. No one touches what's MINE!

XUL

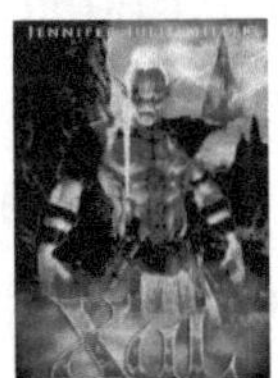

Brittany

All my dreams and wants were stolen from me in the blink of an eye. Awakening, in the middle of a nightmare, I realize I'm being sold like an animal to be studied and dissected in the name of science. Then tragedy strikes, leaving me abandoned and sick. I am only moments from taking my last breath when strong arms pull me from the darkness. I thought it was a blessing that he had found me, the green man who had haunted my dreams. I let myself believe, for just one moment, I might find a small piece of happiness in this unknown world. But what is the old saying? *'Don't count your chickens until they hatch!'*

A blood sucking parasite is eating me alive, literally, and no matter what, I'm not going to survive this horror story. My body is failing me. I beg him to let me go; I just want the pain to stop, but he won't listen. He holds me down and I struggle weakly against his immense strength, choking as blood fills my lungs. When I can't fight any more, Death opens its arms and invites me in.

XuL

My harsh, brutal features have deterred all females, no matter the species. I long for companionship and love. Then I find her, my Kismet, the only one made just for me. The one precious thing I would worship above all others. But the fates are cruel, especially to a male like me.

I am being forced to destroy the fragile bond that has formed between us, as I have to make the hardest decision of my life. One that will make me lose her either way. I hold her small, struggling body against me. Tears flow down my face as she begs me to stop. My heart is crushed as I watch the light leave her beautiful eyes. Upon her final breath, I vow not even Death will keep what's mine.

SOL

Alana

The question is, do I allow this dark moment in time to rob me of the life I could possibly have here? I have never known such horror or fear. If I hadn't experienced it myself, I would have never believed any other living thing could possibly do this to another. The scars may be gone on the outside now, but they will remain forever in my soul. They tell me I can never go back, all that I have ever known is gone. Where does this leave me in the world of monsters? He beckons me, promising me...the fairy-tale... the impossible dream. Everything I have ever wanted to hear! But I don't know if I'm strong enough to go forward as long as the shadows of our past pull me backwards.

SoL

I knew she was withholding the truth from me. I had no idea who I held in my arms until it was almost too late. The moment her true essence was revealed to me, my body reacted, reaching out for the one thing I had been searching for my whole life… my Inamorata. The very mistress of my heart and now that I have finally found her. I will follow her through the sands of time… no matter how long it takes. I will find my way back to her… because she is MINE!

RAZ

Katherine

How do you go on when all of your wants and dreams have been destroyed? My loved ones were snatched right out of my hands, leaving me alone in a world of unknowns and terror. I'm lost in the in-between with no familiar paths to follow until the sound of a heartbeat and a whisper draws me back to the land of the living.

RaZ

The moment I laid eyes upon her face, I knew there would be no distance I wouldn't travel to make her my own. Unknown forces try to steal her from my very arms and even if I have to fight the very essence of her world, the universe, or the very Gods we pray to. Nothing will stop me from making her MINE!

TORDAN

Luna

They stole my dreams, my hopes, my very identity, and I had no idea. Years went by and I did everything I was told, I was always the perfect specimen, and the perfect lab rat. I was dissected, even maimed all in the name of science. Then one day a strange smoky voice entered my head, and I knew things were not as they seemed. He promises me that he will never leave me, but my new memories tell me differently.

Tordan

What is it about that one person that attracts you like no other? My mind can't figure out that riddle, but the moment I laid eyes upon her I knew my life would never be the same. When I finally held her in my arms, I swore I would never be without her again.

If they think they will get me to comply by using her to control me, they're right. What they don't know is…I will tear this compound, and all that's in it apart, to protect what's MINE.

HUGO

Miya

I awaken to the touch of cold metal hands and talking holograms. Paralyzed and dependent on the Others. They tell me a story… at first; I refuse to believe. A story of no return and extreme loss, but one of the voices is different. He projects anger and distrust…but his hands… even though cold and hard, are always gentle. I have come to crave the sound of his growls because I know within moments he will hold me in his arms. When my sight returns. I was not prepared to see what he really was, but when he collapsed in front of me, his body failing. Why do I suddenly feel like this is my biggest loss yet?

Hugo

I have done everything in my power to prepare a safe world for her once I'm gone. I fought my attraction, knowing I was unworthy of her trust, but I crave her like no other. Unfortunately, my mind is no longer my own, and the only way to destroy the monster who has invaded my head is death. All that matters in my end... is that she survives... because I would rather die than share what I know is MINE.

PLAYBOY AND THE WAITRESS

Jenna

I was always told never to forget that I was worth something, too! We all know that every little girl dreams of her knight in shining armor. A man who will ride up and save her from the evil things trying to destroy her. Then, of course, we all know they live happily ever after. My knight was untouchable… A Playboy, a man who stole my heart right out of my chest and with very little effort on his part. Unfortunately, he was also a man whose world I would never fit in. You can take the girl out of the country. You can dress her in nice clothes, have her smile beautifully as you parade her on your arm, but you never really take the country out of the girl. I reach out for the brightest of stars… only for him to leave my heart in pieces, crumbling at my feet.

Dage

I watched her for weeks. Every smile she bestowed on me captured me in a way no others had. Circumstances throw us together over and over and no matter how many times I hold her in my arms, it's never enough. I didn't know what I was missing until she walked away. I know, I can't have them and her… so who will lose?

www.ingramcontent.com/pod-product-compliance
Lightning Source LLC
Chambersburg PA
CBHW021344150726
47989CB00005B/2101